THE ROMANCE OF HERALDRY

BY THE SAME AUTHOR

CIVIC HERALDRY OF ENGLAND AND WALES

SHAKESPEARE'S HERALDRY

LOOKING AT HERALDRY

THE ROMANCE OF HERALDRY

by

C. WILFRID SCOTT-GILES, O.B.E., M.A. (Cantab.)

FITZALAN PURSUIVANT OF ARMS EXTRAORDINARY
FELLOW OF THE HERALDRY SOCIETY

Illustrated by the Author

LONDON: J. M. DENT & SONS LIMITED
NEW YORK: E. P. DUTTON & CO. INC.

TO MY

MOTHER AND FATHER

CONTENTS

LIST OF ILLUSTRATIONS

PREFACE

To John Brooke-Little, Esq.,
    Bluemantle Pursuivant of Arms,
    Chairman of the Heraldry Society.

My dear Bluemantle,

    A number of members of the Heraldry Society have told me that this book was their first introduction to heraldry, and aroused their lasting interest in the subject. Some of them have been good enough to indicate matters needing correction or modification, and I have adopted their suggestions where possible, though practical considerations prevent extensive revision.

    It is not to be expected that I should be entirely satisfied with a book which I wrote thirty-five years ago. If I were writing it to-day, there are some things I should put differently. But on the whole I think the book captures the spirit of heraldry, and presents the subject in a way likely to interest those with no prior knowledge. It is gratifying to know that the demand for the book calls for a fifth printing, and I hope it may continue to lead many of its readers on to further study.

    I am always pleased to correspond with fellow students, whether members of the Society or not.

Yours sincerely,
C. W. Scott-Giles,
Fitzalan
Pursuivant Extraordinary.

3 Branstone Road,
    Kew Gardens.
       October 1964.

FIG. I.—STRIP OF THE SYON COPE.

THE ROMANCE OF HERALDRY

I

" THE SHORTHAND OF HISTORY "

" Would not a general knowledge of the arms of our principal ancient English families form a sort of artificial memory for the young student of English history, and give additional interest to the details of the deeds of those who bore them : of events in which the founders of those families were actors? "—J. R. Planché, *Pursuivant of Arms.*

IN the days of chivalry heralds were concerned with the conduct of tournaments, announcing the champions and acclaiming the victor. In war they carried challenges, noted the men of rank present at a battle, and those lying dead after it. To carry out these duties they had to be familiar with the signs on shields and flags which knights began to use in the twelfth century so that, when armed and helmed, they might be known one from another. Having this knowledge, heralds could advise a warrior what sign he might assume without duplicating one already in use. In due course the principal heralds were empowered to devise and grant such cognisances.

When full armour ceased to be used, and tournaments were no longer held, the original functions of the heralds came to an end; but men continued to use, on seals, monuments, and the decoration of their houses, the insignia inherited from their ancestors, while new-comers to the nobility and gentry also sought these tokens of honour. The control of armorial bearings, together with the recording of pedigrees, then became the chief business of the heralds.

Heraldry survives to-day as a decorative and emblematic art, retaining

B
1

the knightly shield and helm as its traditional basis. It has become increasingly symbolic, containing many allusions to personal, national, and local history.   It has also retained something of its original purpose as a means of recognition, for in two great wars signs have been extensively used in the field to identify the men, transport, and equipment of military divisions and units; while ships of the Royal Navy, and squadrons of the Royal Air Force, also have their heraldic badges.

Limitations of Heraldry.

This book deals in a popular manner with heraldry as " the shorthand of history," but in quoting that phrase of Planché's we must not overlook on the one hand the limitations of heraldry, and on the other the dimensions of history. The popular idea that every coat-of-arms has a symbolic meaning is false; it is not true of heraldry that " every picture tells a story." The decoration of shields, which has been a persistent custom among warlike people in all ages, was in mediæval Europe systematised into what we now call heraldry to meet a definite need, namely, to provide warriors when fully armed with a means of identification. Shut in his house of steel, the knight felt much the same need to hang out a name-plate that a householder feels to-day, but in an age when few could read, the knight's sign was of necessity pictorial rather than written, especially as it had to be clearly recognisable at a distance; while the desire for decorative effect had also to be satisfied.

In early heraldry the utilitarian motive prevailed, and symbolism was a matter of secondary importance. Few ancient coats-of-arms were devised with the express intention of telling something of the owner's history or character, though in modern times many fables have been invented by vainglorious owners of old coats to account for their hereditary emblems—as if the right to bear such antique marks of honour were not in itself sufficient cause for just pride. These baseless family legends have been responsible for the general misconception that all arms are essentially symbolical; I have repeated

FIG. 2.—SEAL OF JOHN DE WARRENNE, EARL OF SURREY, *showing identification value of heraldry to the armed knight.*

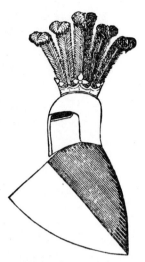

FIG. 3.—WALDEGRAVE: *Parti-coloured shield and panache.*

a few of them partly for their romantic interest, and partly because of the shreds of history which cling to them, but chiefly as instances of stories which should be politely received and privately discredited.

A true perspective of heraldry can best be obtained by briefly examining some of the motives which in the age of chivalry led men to adopt their particular cognisances, and the factors which in later times produced changes and developments in coats-of-arms.

The shields recorded in the early rolls of arms, or heraldic catalogues (which began to be compiled in the thirteenth century), fall into two main classes : those which seem to have had a casual rather than a causal origin; and those which were devised to denote the name, family or feudal connections or office of the user. With the latter class of arms we shall be chiefly concerned, since they are to some extent historical records. At the former we need only glance.

Arms of Casual Origin.

The plain shield of Waldegrave, "parted palewise" (divided vertically) into white and red, provides us with an example of a small group of arms in which distinction is obtained merely by parti-colouring (Fig. 3).

The simple geometrical designs (ordinaries) such as the chief (head of the shield), fesse (*fascia*, the girth or central horizontal stripe), bend (diagonal stripe), chevron (inverted V), and pale (vertical stripe) are shown in Fig. 4. Except the cross and saltire, which have religious associations, these forms have no particular significance, but were adopted only for identification. In some cases arms of this type may have been produced by colouring the bands of metal added to a shield to strengthen it; banded and studded shields occur in the pre-heraldic Bayeux Tapestry (Fig. 48). Since boldness was essential in arms, so that they might be clearly seen at a distance, contrasting tinctures were used, and it became the rule that a gold object should not be placed on a silver shield, but that metals and colours should be effectively mingled.

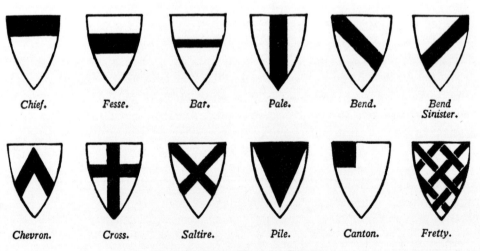

Chief.   Fesse.   Bar.   Pale.   Bend.   Bend Sinister.

Chevron.   Cross.   Saltire.   Pile.   Canton.   Fretty.

FIG. 4.—SIMPLE HERALDIC FORMS.

The shield of a branch of the Montgomery family provides an example of arms which sprang from the emblem on an early seal. John Mundegumbri, in the twelfth century, had a single fleur-de-lys on his seal, and this was developed into three golden fleurs-de-lys upon blue in the shield of his descendants. (These arms are identical but have no connection with the Royal Arms of France.)

Obviously arms which arose in these haphazard ways can have no primary historic significance, though many of them acquired historical associations through the careers of their users. Let us turn to the heraldic emblems in the choice of which a definite purpose can be traced.

Arms with a Meaning.

Foremost in this class are arms which bear out our analogy of the name-plate on the modern front door, seeking to express the name of their owner in pictorial form. Many men who bore a name which was capable of heraldic illustration devised punning arms. Instances which readily occur to the mind are bull of Bovill, the trumpets of Trumpington, the roach of Roche, the whelk shells of Shelley, and so on. The reader may guess at the principal charges in the arms of the families of Salmon, Herring, Talbot, Wolf, Rabbett and Heron. A less obvious example is the portcullis (*windy gate*) in the arms of Wingate or Windegate.

The accompanying page of illustrations (Figs. 5–13) provides sufficient other examples to show that in seeking the origin of early coats-of-arms, the pun theory should have first consideration. In some of these instances the play on the name is rather obscure. The fretty design (Fig. 5) represents a *herring net* when (silver on black) it stands for Harrington; while (gold on black) for Maltravers it represents something *hard to pass*. The charges in Fig. 6 are heraldic chess-rooks. Fig. 8 shows a whirlpool or *gurges*. The three objects in Fig. 11 are *maunches* (sleeves). The sword, as the emblem of St. Paul, is appropriate to Paulet; while Molyneux bears a *fer-de-moline*, the iron fastener at the centre of a mill wheel.

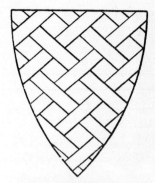

FIG. 5.—HARRINGTON AND
MALTRAVERS.

FIG. 6.—ROOKWOOD.

FIG. 7.—TREMAYNE.

FIG. 8.—GORGES.

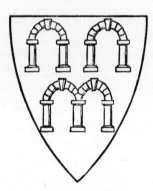

FIG. 9.—ARCHES.

FIG. 10.—TRUMPINGTON.

FIG. 11.—MAUNSELL.

FIG. 12.—PAULET.

FIG. 13.—MOLYNEUX.

PUNNING HERALDRY

FIG. 14.—ARGENTON.

FIG. 15.—GRAND CHAMPION OF ENGLAND.

What a commentary upon mediæval knighthood is John Dennis's dictum, " He that will make a pun will pick a pocket ! "

Some arms were devised to record the incidents of feudal tenure. For instance, the family of Argenton, who once held the manor of Wimondley, which entailed that the tenant should present a cup of wine to the King at his coronation, bore three silver covered cups on a red shield (Fig. 14). Sir John Argenton performed this service at the coronation of Richard II, and had the silver cup for his fee.

As an example of official coats we have the silver sword on a black shield attaching to the office of Hereditary Grand Champion of England (Fig. 15). This was formerly borne by the Marmions, whose descendant and successor to the Championship, the head of the family of Dymoke, still quarters it with his own arms; while his motto, *Pro Rege dimico*, " I fight for the King," happily combines a play upon his name with a reference to his office. The desire to suggest their name—at least its second syllable—led the ancient Dymokes to adopt as a crest " two asses eerys grey." One admires their disregard of possible ridicule more than the sensitiveness of some of their successors, who have robbed their crest of significance by substituting the scalp and ears of a hare for those of a moke.

Since the flowering of heraldry occurred at a time when feudalism was at its height, it naturally happened that many men acknowledged their feudal dependency by basing their arms upon those of their overlord, introducing necessary differences of colour and detail. For

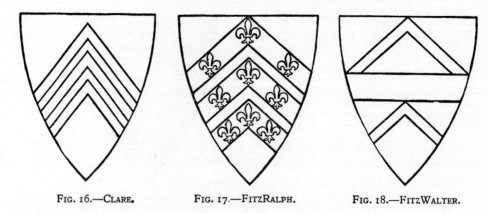

FIG. 16.—CLARE.   FIG. 17.—FITZRALPH.   FIG. 18.—FITZWALTER.

instance, the cinquefoil (perhaps a punning pimpernel) of FitzPernell, Earl of Leicester, is found in the arms of several old Leicestershire families, and still forms the arms of the city of Leicester.   Three chevrons derived from the arms of the great house of Clare (three red chevrons upon gold—Fig. 16), variously coloured and sometimes borne with other emblems, appear in the arms of many families which were connected with them feudally, such as the FitzRalphs, who placed three fleurs-de-lys upon each chevron (Fig. 17).

Similarity of arms may, therefore, denote an ancient feudal connection between the families which bear them.   It may also indicate that the families sprang from the same stock.   For instance, the arms of the FitzWalters, two chevrons and a fess of red upon gold (Fig. 18), recall that this family traced their ancestry to Robert, fifth son of Richard de Tonbridge, Earl of Clare.   Further examples will be found in Chapter VII.

Thus far the meanings which have been shown to attach to some classes of arms relate only to personal, family or feudal affairs, and are unconnected with national events.   But in the latter years of the age of chivalry, heraldry began to reflect historical occurrences, as kings and princes came to mark signal services on the part of certain of their followers by the grant of significant arms, or of augmentations —the addition of honourable emblems to existing shields.   Still later, as the original purpose of heraldry as a means of identification ceased, owing to changed methods of warfare and the abandonment of complete body armour, the symbolical side of the art-science was developed to a greater extent, and to-day a very large number of newly-created coats-of-arms contain some reference to the status, profession or achievements of the men to whom they are granted.

Elaboration of Arms.

The monumental tombs in our churches have made us familiar with shields divided into many compartments, known as quarterings. The practice of marshalling several coats-of-arms on one shield arose from a desire to denote important marriage alliances. When a man marries an heiress or co-heiress of an armorial family, he may incorporate her arms permanently in his own shield, and transmit them to his descendants. He adds not only her paternal coat, but also any quarterings which may have accrued to it in the past. In this manner many present-day families carry in their arms a heraldic record of a number of ancient families, their more or less remote ancestors, whose names may have long since died out. An elaborately quartered shield is often far less artistic than a simple and less pretentious coat ; but it is historically of much greater interest, because it is an index to the former status and fortunes of the family which bears it.

The arms of Gregory Fiennes, Lord Dacre of the South, who died in 1594 (Fig. 19) are an example of this method of marshalling. They indicate that the members of the family of Fiennes had married the heiresses of noble houses, whose ancestors had in their turn married other heiresses ; so that Gregory bore beside his own paternal lions the arms of Dacre, Multon, Vaux, Morville, FitzHugh, Stavely, Furneaux, Grey, Marmion, St. Quentin and Gernegan. Lord Dacre left no children, but his noble display of heraldry survives in the arms of Emanuel School, founded by his widow.

The illustration of these arms shows how metals and colours are denoted in heraldic drawings. A plain surface represents white or silver (*argent*) ; dots mean gold (*or*) ; vertical lines, red (*gules*) ; horizontal lines, blue (*azure*) ; diagonal lines, left to right downwards, green (*vert*) ; and diagonals in the other direction, purple (*purpure*). Where there is an accompanying description (or blazon) of the arms,

Or (gold)

Argent (silver)

Sable (black)

Gules (red)

Azure (blue)

Vert (green)

FIG. 19.—ARMS OF GREGORY FIENNES, LORD DACRE
OF THE SOUTH (*now borne by* EMANUEL SCHOOL),
*showing marshalling of quarterings to denote ancestry,
and method of indicating heraldic tinctures by dots and
lines.*

these indications (which somewhat detract from the simple beauty of the heraldic forms) are unnecessary, and are generally omitted in this book. This system of indicating tinctures was not introduced until the seventeenth century.

Heraldry and Personal Honour.

To-day most people who possess a shield-of-arms regard it as no more than an interesting relic of an ancestral past; privately they may feel a sense of satisfaction in such evidence of gentle forbears, but personal heraldry is no longer indicative of class or privilege. In earlier times, however, " the coat armour of every house was a precious inheritance, which descended, under definite limitations and with distinct differences, to every member of the family : a man's shield proved his gentle or noble birth, illustrated his pedigree, and put him on his honour not to disgrace the bearings which his noble progenitors had worn " (Stubbs). The shield-of-arms was the shrine of personal honour, as closely associated with its owner as his very name, and a man was doubly disgraced who suffered armorial degradation; witness the case, in the reign of Edward II, of the two Lords Despenser, who were purposely clad in their coat armour before they were hanged, drawn and quartered.

The right to the exclusive use of a particular coat-of-arms was jealously guarded. When, in 1375, Sir Richard le Scrope and Sir Robert Grosvenor were found to be using the same arms, namely, a golden bend upon blue, since pride forbade that either should voluntarily relinquish them, their dispute came before Richard II in the court of chivalry. Grosvenor lost the case, and had therefore to change his arms. A suggestion that he should do so by simply placing a silver border round the bend was regarded as insufficient, since it would seem to be merely one of those minor additions assumed by junior members of a family to denote cadency. It was required that Grosvenor should entirely abandon the bend, and Grosvenor thereupon took for arms a golden wheatsheaf upon blue, derived from the arms of the old Earldom of Chester. The wheatsheaf is still borne by the Duke of Westminster.

Heraldry and History.

I have been at pains to show that heraldry, as " the shorthand of history," has distinct limitations, and these are the more narrow because the term history is capable of wide extension. In a small sense history is but the literary expression of a man's " natural joy in great actions and great events "; but the modern historian is not content merely to chronicle events; he looks beneath them for under-lying movements of which the happenings themselves are but symptoms, and the study of history becomes not an end in itself, but the means to the fuller understanding of the development and destiny of mankind.

Heraldry belongs to the narrower view of history; it is pertinent only to the dramatic and personal element. The economic or con-stitutional historian will find in it little to help him. But whoever reads the chronicles for their own sake, taking interest in dynastic questions, the incidents of warfare, the romance and the personalities, will find in heraldic emblems of nations and of individuals much that will help to make " these dry bones live." For after we have elimin-ated the vast number of arms and badges which have no significance (or none that can be traced) and no historical interest, there yet remain sufficient to illuminate many pages in the history of our land. Some of these have been collected together in this book, arranged in a rough chronological order, and explained as far as possible in non-technical language.

I have permitted myself considerable licence in what I have included in the term heraldry. Strictly speaking, the word embraces all the lore of a herald, of which the supervision of armorial bearings was only one branch. There is no contemporary heraldry to illustrate our history much before the Third Crusade. But for the purposes of historic symbolism I have included the designs upon some ancient coins and traditional standards of the Romans, Britons and Saxons, and (in later times) historical medals which, though beyond the sphere of heraldry, are related to it.

Students of heraldry will be familiar with all the historic arms and devices which are here recorded, and I have only to ask their tolerant consideration of the few original theories that I advance. It is to general readers that this book is addressed; it is, in fact, not so much an addition to the bibliography of heraldry as a book of history treated from the heraldic point of view. I hope it may encourage some historical students to give more attention to heraldry; but if they wish to do so they must go to more technical and more complete books, and learn something of the grammar and laws of the science. Meanwhile may this book serve as an introduction—I hope an attractive one.

The arms in the strip of the Syon Cope reproduced at the head of this chapter are as follows:

(i) Vaire of gold and red, a blue border charged with sixteen silver horseshoes, for William Ferrers, fifth Earl of Derby. (The horseshoes bear punning reference to his surname.)

(ii) Three open horse-breys of gold upon blue; on an ermine chief a half-lion of red, for Geneville.

(iii) Gold and blue chequers; a red bend with three golden lions, for John de Clifford.

(iv) Silver and red quarters, with a gold fret upon red, and a black bend over all, for Le Despenser.

(v) A gold Agnus Dei with a white banner, upon red,—a badge of the Knights Templars.

FIG. 20.—COIN OF THE EMPEROR HADRIAN :
The Watch on the Wall.

FIG. 21.—MEDAL OF CHARLES II :
The Watch on the Sea Frontier.

II

ROMA DEA AND BRITANNIA

" We saw great Roma Dea atop of the wall, the frost on her helmet, and her spear pointed towards the North Star."—Kipling, *Puck of Pook's Hill.*

THE emblems which illustrate the history of our land begin many centuries before the development of a systematised heraldry such as we have to-day, the earliest examples being found in the designs on coins and standards of the Romans and Anglo-Saxons. Of the use of personal or tribal emblems by the pre-Roman Britons we have but few and doubtful evidences. Whether the woad patterns with which they decorated their bodies formed a crude heraldry ; whether the figures cut on the slopes of our chalk hills have any symbolic meaning, we cannot tell. The few ancient coins which have endured are merely debased copies of the coinage of the civilised Mediterranean countries, and contain no emblems which can be regarded as characteristically British.

But of the Roman occupation of Britain and the Roman-British resistance to the Anglo-Saxon invaders we possess a few reminders— the modern arms of some towns, the " tail " side of the pennies, and the badge of Wales.

14

The arms of Wallsend are a black shield with golden drops, and therein a masoned wall upon which stands a golden eagle (Fig. 22). Thus Wallsend commemorates the days when she was Segedunum of the Romans—at the end of the wall whence the Imperial eagle held watch against the northern barbarians—and at the same time tells of her present-day industries, the black field with its golden drops being clearly intended to denote the collieries and copper-smelting works.

When Emperor Hadrian built his wall between Wallsend and Carlisle, he commemorated the event by issuing coins which bore the figure of a woman, clad in draperies and wearing a helmet, and armed with a spear and an oval shield (Fig. 20). This figure, which (according to the exhibit in the British Museum) represents the Roman Watch on the Wall, is probably not a personal Britannia—the inscribed name appears to be only that of the Province—but represents Roma Dea, the symbolic personification of the Roman State. Her very evanescence in the symbolism of our land is of historic significance, for Roma left few influences in Britain. Her most lasting heritage was the road system. This has heraldic record in the arms of Cheshunt, and of Kesteven (Lincs.) County Council, in which an ermine pale represents Ermine Street, which passed through these places.

Roma Dea disappeared from Britain with the Roman legions, but after a lapse of twelve centuries the armed female figure reappeared on our coins and medals. Meanwhile the "painted people" north of the Wall had come to be called Scots, after an invading tribe from

FIG. 22.—WALLSEND (*Segedunum*): *The Roman Eagle at the Wall's End, with a coal-black background.*

Ireland, and a king of Scottish birth had ascended the English throne. Roma Dea's successor, Britannia, was therefore represented as maintaining her watch not upon the Wall, but upon the sea frontier. John Roettiers, engraver to the Mint in the reign of Charles II, who executed the medal represented in Fig. 21, took for his model the famous beauty Frances Theresa Stuart, afterwards Duchess of Richmond; " and a pretty thing it is," wrote Pepys, " that he should choose *her* face to represent Britannia by."

The Dragon of Wales.

Some of the Roman coins, and copies thereof, remained in use in Britain after the withdrawal of the legions, and it is at least possible that the Roman symbols continued to be used by the Britons, and particularly by those who, being of Latin blood (though they may never have seen Rome), naturally clung to the Roman tradition. Foremost among these emblems was the Imperial eagle, the standard of the legion; but while this was the ancestor of the German, Russian, Austrian and Polish eagles, it did not provide Britain with a national emblem.

On the other hand, the dragon, the standard of the cohort, has had a practically uninterrupted career in these islands from the Roman conquest to the present day. In Europe, the dragon was originally a Dacian emblem. It was adopted by the Romans after Trajan's conquest of Dacia early in the second century, and brought into Britain as a military ensign. Here it stood as an emblem of authority and power for at least two centuries. Did it then vanish with the legions, or did it linger to lead the Britons in the wars against the Saxon invaders? It certainly seems to have been an emblem of Cadwallader, who lived within two centuries of the Roman withdrawal, and it is attributed to the more remote and shadowy line of kings which culminated in the glorious King Arthur.

According to legend, Uther, the father of Arthur, saw two golden dragons in the sky, and took them as an omen that he should attain to the Kingship. He subsequently caused two such dragons to be made, and dedicated one to the church at Winchester, while the other

FIG. 23.—BADGE OF WALES.   FIG. 24.—SOMERSET.

THE ROMANO-BRITISH DRAGON.

he bore as his standard in battle. His title of Pendragon, or " dragon-head," suggests the use of the emblem as some kind of a crest.

Supposing this legend to be of real antiquity, it indicates that in that confused period when Britons and Saxons strove for the possession of a land vacated by Rome, the dragon was an emblem of leadership among the defenders; and it requires little argument to connect " the dragon of the great Pendragonship " with the derelict standard of the Roman cohorts.

This suggestion accords with the theory that the chieftain who is celebrated by the name of Arthur, whom the ancient Welsh writers call *yr amherawdyr* (*imperator*), and who succeeded as *dux bellorum* in uniting some of the British tribes against the Saxons, was a Roman Briton who took to himself the vacant Imperial title. Such a man would most probably have adopted the historic and familiar Roman emblem as his standard.

It should, however, be noticed that Nennius, the seventh-century Abbot of Bangor—or possibly someone who wrote in his name at a later time—attributed to Arthur a shield containing the definitely Christian emblems of a cross and an image of the Virgin; while another Arthurian chronicler tells us that his banners were " inlaid with gules and with crowns of gold fairly adorned."

The red dragon holding a blue mace—the emblem of local

C

government—stands in the golden shield of the Somerset County Council (Fig. 24), in token that the county claims to have been the centre of King Arthur's realm, containing "many towered Camelot," the name of which survives in Queen's Camel; and Avalon, which is Glastonbury.

If the British dragon may be identified with the Roman cohort standard, it follows that *y ddraig goch*, the red dragon which is still the badge of Wales (Fig. 23) is a descendant of the emblem of Imperial Rome.   The dragon appears in the arms or badges of several old Welsh families, notably the Tudors, who, when they ascended the English throne in the person of Henry VII, restored the red dragon to its ancient status as a royal emblem.   It remains to this day in the arms of Cardiff (Fig. 25) and other Welsh corporations, and of some Cornish towns.

The Welsh Leek.

Another emblem which tradition associates with British resistance to the Saxons is the leek, which Cadwallader, at the suggestion of St. David, is said to have ordered his men to wear in their caps as a cognisance in battle.

In *Henry V*, Shakespeare puts into the mouth of Fluellen words which seem to imply that in his day the emblem of the leek was thought to have originated at Poictiers, where

> " the Welshmen did good service in a garden where leeks did grow, wearing leeks in their Monmouth caps ; which, your majesty know, to this hour is an honourable badge of the service ; and I do believe your majesty takes no scorn to wear the leek upon St. Tavy's day."

But there is a hint of the older legend when Fluellen demands that Pistol shall eat the leek he has maligned, and Pistol refuses in the words :

> " Not for Cadwallader and all his goats."

The leek grows in the shield of Cardiff previously referred to (Fig. 25), which is supported by a goat and a sea-horse. These arms were granted in 1906. Since then the theory has gained ground that "St. Peter's Leek" (the daffodil) rather than the vegetable leek is the proper emblem of Wales, and the flower represents Wales in the present issue of postage stamps. The flower may be the pleasanter emblem, but thanks to Shakespeare it is to the leek that the flavour of romance belongs.

FIG. 25.—CARDIFF.
*The Welsh dragon, the leek, and the banner
of the Lords of Glamorgan.*

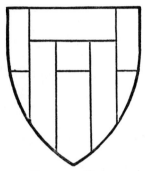

FIG. 25a.—CHUBB.
*An heraldic representation
of Stonehenge.*

Antiquities.

We may here notice some armorial bearings which refer to archaeological or antiquarian remains.

Maidstone's shield is supported by the Borough's "oldest inhabitant"—an iguanodon whose complete skeleton was dug up in the town. Farnham has in its crest a stone-headed axe, and the arms of some other towns also allude to antiquities.

One of the triliths of Stonehenge is shown in heraldic form in the arms of Chubb (Fig. 25a), the first baronet of that name having presented Stonehenge to the nation. The chief and pales representing the stones are white, and the background is blue and green for sky and grass.

FIG. 26.—KENT.
The white horse of " Hengist and Horsa."

FIG. 27.—WEST SUSSEX.
The " hirondelles " of the Arundels.

FIG. 28.—MIDDLESEX.
The Saxon seaxes.

III

THE STANDARDS OF THE ENGLISH

" The conflict of banners,
 the clash of spears,
 the meeting of the heroes
 and the rustling of weapons."
Anglo-Saxon Chronicle.

WITH the coming of the English we find ourselves on firmer ground historically, but not yet free from the marshes of heraldic conjecture. Our period is, of course, still pre-heraldic; yet we know that banners were used in Saxon England. At the battle of Brumby, for instance,

" The sons of Edward
 their board walls clove
 and hewed their banners
 with the wrecks of their hammers."
Anglo-Saxon Chronicle.

And Bede tells us of the East Anglian King Edwin, that " his dignity was so great throughout his dominions that his banners were not only borne before him in battle, but even in time of peace, when he rode about his cities, towns or provinces, with his officers, the standard-bearer was wont to go before him."

20

Across the centuries we descry the banners of these old kings, but for the most part we cannot discern the emblems they display. Only the Kentish Horse, the Wessex Dragon and the Danish Raven are clear to the eye.

Yet the heralds of the Middle Ages, tantalised by these glimpses, did not hesitate to credit the Anglo-Saxon realms with fully-developed coats-of-arms, and as these have survived to the present day in the shields of various counties and towns, religious and educational foundations, they deserve some attention as indirect pointers to our early history.

The White Horse of Kent.

The arms of the County of Kent tell us of the first Teutonic settlement on British shores.

Dear to the literary historians are those stormy petrels of the Anglo-Saxon invaders, Hengist and Horsa, and we may be somewhat loth to dispose of them. But it seems to be established that the famous brothers are mythical. The names Hengist and Horsa are synonymous, both meaning " the Horse." " The White Horse was the ensign of the invaders," states Dr. Donaldson (*English Ethnography*). " The Frisians called it their Hengist, and the Anglians their Horsa."

" Hengist and Horsa," therefore, were one Saxon chieftain whose emblem was a horse. We may accept the statement of the *Anglo-Saxon Chronicle*, that this chieftain claimed descent from Odin : it was no uncommon boast (though the monkish writers thought it necessary to disguise the pagan ancestry of the English kings by converting the All-Father into a human hero, whose descent was traceable, through Noah, to Adam).

Now, one of the attributes of Odin was the horse Sleipner, and it is possible that it was this beast that the Anglo-Frisian standard represented. It is certainly true that white horses had a special significance to the invaders. They played a part in religious ceremonies, and their neighing was taken as a presage of the outcome of battles. Whatever the origin of this horse, its subsequent history is

clear.   It became the emblem of the Kingdom of Kent, founded by
the chieftain whom we know as Hengist, and to this day ramps upon
a red shield in the arms of the County of Kent (Fig. 26); it also
figures in the arms of several Kentish boroughs such as Ramsgate,
Margate (Fig. 118), Bromley, Erith and Lewisham.

One of the most remarkable manifestations of the white horse in
modern times is as the trade-mark on steam-rollers produced by a
Kentish firm.   Adopting the emblem of Kent, the firm have broken
in the steed which was wont to permit none but Odin to mount him;
and the white horse has become a servitor in the land to which he
came as a conqueror.

The white horse remained the standard of the peoples from which
the English sprang, and is found to-day in the shield of Westphalia,
identical with that of Kent.   As will be seen later in this book, during
the reigns of the Hanoverian kings it appeared in our Royal Arms as
part of the arms of the Electorate of Hanover.

While I believe we are on safe ground in deriving the Kentish
horse from the Anglo-Saxon invaders, reference should be made to
the contrary theory which connects it with the white horses of pre-
Saxon and even pre-Roman times—the horses cut in the chalk downs,
and stamped on the coins of more than one British king, and possibly
connected with ancient sun-cults.

The Sussex Swallows.

Hard on the hoofs of the Jutish white horse came Saxon Ælla,
who landed at Anderida (Pevensey) and won the chalk downs for his
own.   Ælla founded the colony of South Saxons, which were credited
by the thirteenth-century heralds with a banner containing six birds,
known in heraldry as martlets.   But in reality this device is only
traceable to the Norman family, de Arundel, which assumed arms
consisting of six swallows, or *hirondelles*, in punning allusion to their
name.   These arms came to be regarded as the ancient banner of the
Sussex kingdom.

The crest of the town of Arundel contains a swallow.   The

six martlets appear in the arms of the West Sussex County Council (Fig. 27), and have been incorporated in the arms of several towns, such as Brighton, Hove and Bexhill.

The Golden Dragon of Wessex.

The West Saxons, who first made their appearance under Cerdic in 495, when they landed near Southampton, adopted a golden dragon for their standard. This people encountered the organised resistance of the British chieftains, and if the latter really cherished the dragon as their emblem, the West Saxons in choosing a like monster may have intended to signify their victory over the British. If, as some Celtic writers assert, the Welsh dragon was originally not red, but of " ruddy gold," there is additional reason for thinking that the dragon of Wessex was derived from that of the Britons.

Henry of Huntingdon mentions the dragon standard as having been borne by Cuthred of Wessex in the battle of Burford in 752, when he triumphed over the Mercians. The golden dragon was certainly raised by Harold at Hastings, for it is twice represented in the Bayeux Tapestry (Fig. 48). The dragon continued to be held in high regard after the Norman Conquest, remaining " the customary standard of English kings." We shall meet it again in the following chapter.

The Seaxes.

The arms of the counties of Middlesex (Fig. 28) and Essex contain the three notched swords, or *seaxes*, which are traditionally supposed to have been the emblems of the East Saxons. There is an old theory that the Saxons derived their name from the use of this weapon, as the Scythians from the scimitar.

The writer of the continuation of Florence of Worcester's Chronicle evidently had this idea in mind when he narrated that a " foreign and savage " race in old times came from the north and settled in Thuringia. Growing in strength, they refused tribute. A conference was called, to which the strangers came, " carrying secretly long sheathed knives,"

FIG. 29.—BURY ST. EDMUNDS.

FIG. 30.—ISLE OF ELY COUNTY COUNCIL.

FIG. 31.—EAST ANGLIA.

FIG. 32.—OXFORD UNIVERSITY.

FIG. 33.—COLCHESTER.

with which they attacked the native Thuringians; and the land, "which up to that time had been called Thuringia, was afterwards by a change of name called Saxony, from these long and victorious knives."

Ealing, Fulham and other boroughs of Middlesex and Essex incorporate the seaxes in their arms; and it is somewhat incongruous to find emblems of such bloody memories on so peaceful a thing as a Corporation vehicle.

The English Crowns.

Behind the Saxons came their near relatives, the Angles, to whom the heralds assigned as arms three golden crowns on blue (Fig. 31) which still have heraldic usage in East Anglia. The same design occurs in Scandinavia as the arms of Sweden, and this may tempt us to suppose that the heralds of the Middle Ages, in devising arms for the old East Anglian kingdom, gave it the shield of Sweden, knowing the people to have been of Scandinavian stock; but the arms of Sweden do not appear to go back far enough for this, and the resemblance seems to have no significance.

To St. Edmund, the last East Anglian king, who received martyrdom at the hands of the Danes, the heralds assigned the three crowns, each pierced by two arrows, and these emblems, upon blue (Fig. 29), to this day form the arms of Bury St. Edmunds. The crest of the town, a wolf holding the crowned and severed head of the martyred king, relates to a legend that after Edmund's death his followers found his body less the head. Their search for the head was directed by the dead king's voice crying, " Here, here! " until they came upon it guarded by a wolf.

The arms of several places in eastern England recall the old East Anglian kingdom. Three gold crowns on red, the shield of the See of Ely, tells that the old fenland monastery was founded by a lady of the royal house, St. Etheldreda, whose name, corrupted to St. Audrey, gave us the word " tawdry," first applied to the goods sold at St. Audrey's fair.

The Isle of Ely County Council bears St. Etheldreda's gold crowns on a red pile, the background being barry wavy silver and blue, the heraldic representation of water, here alluding to the fen country. The crest consists of a hand grasping a gold trident entwined by an eel —an emblem which refers to the supposed derivation of the name from " eel isle," stated by Bede to be due to " the great plenty of eels taken in these marshes " (Fig. 30).

Red upon gold, the crowns stand for St. Osyth, Queen of the East Saxons, who founded a monastery at Chick, in Essex, and was murdered by the Danes in 676.

Three gold crowns with a ragged cross of silver in a red shield are the arms of Colchester (Fig. 33). The crowns are those of the East Angles, but the cross refers to a legend of Roman British times. The Empress Helena, mother of Constantine and daughter of King Cole (the " merry old soul " of the nursery rhyme, who gave the town its name), is said to have discovered the True Cross in the Holy Land, with those of the two malefactors. It was identified by its miraculous power to restore a sick woman to health. Helena had the cross enclosed in silver, and built a magnificent church in Jerusalem in which to keep it. The cross in the arms is identified as the Holy Rood by the three nails. The arms of Nottingham differ from those of Colchester only in having a green cross.

In the Midlands, the three crowns on blue, set about an open book, form the arms of Oxford University, and remind us of the high regard in which St. Edmund was held by the mediæval ecclesiastics who chose his emblems to dignify the great seat of learning (Fig. 32).

Looking further afield, we find the three crowns in the old shield of Ireland and (still retained by the present government) in the present shield of Munster. The crowns crossed the Irish sea in Anglo-Norman times, when the invaders of Ireland set out under the banner of St. Edmund. Heraldry thus provides us with a link between the eastern counties of England and the south-west of Ireland.

The Venerable Bede, monk of Jarrow, who has been quoted, is commemorated in the modern arms of Jarrow by a book inscribed *Beda Historia Ecclesiastica* (Fig. 34).

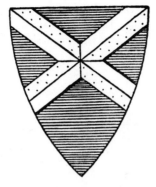

FIG. 34.—JARROW.

FIG. 35.—SEE OF BATH AND WELLS.

FIG. 36.—OFFA'S CROSS
a Divisional sign during the First World War.

Northumbria and Mercia.

Like the Sussex swallows, the ramping lion which the heralds attributed to the old Kingdom of Deira is of no greater antiquity than Norman times, and was taken from the arms of a great local family of the thirteenth century. After the marriage of the heiress of the Percys with Jocelin of Louvain (brother-in-law of Henry I), their descendants, still surnamed Percy, bore in their arms the blue lion on gold of Louvain, which is still included in the shield of the Duke of Northumberland. This emblem the heralds chose to stand for the old kingdom. (An alternative theory derives the lion of the Percys from that of the FitzAlans, consequent on the marriage of Henry, first Lord Percy, with the daughter of FitzAlan, Earl of Arundel, about 1299.)

To the neighbouring Kingdom of Bernicia the heralds assigned a vertically striped gold and red (or purple) banner, perhaps based on Bede's reference to " a banner made of gold and purple " which was hung over King Oswald's tomb at Bardney.

The silver and gold saltire upon blue of the See of Bath and Wells (Fig. 35) is probably based on the saltire which the heralds supposed to have been the emblem of the Kingdom of Mercia, Bath Abbey being the descendant of a College founded by the Mercian King Offa. The gold saltire on blue of the city of St. Albans also

FIG. 37.—ST. AUGUSTINE.

FIG. 38.—PROVINCE OF CAN-
TERBURY.

FIG. 42.—SEE OF DURHAM,
commemorating ST. OSWALD. *The plume and
coronet indicate the Palatinate jurisdiction.*

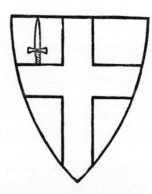

FIG. 39.—SEE OF LONDON.
The swords of ST. PAUL.

FIG. 40.—CITY OF LONDON.
The cross of ST. GEORGE
and the sword of ST. PAUL.

FIG. 41.—SEE OF ROCHESTER.
The saltire of ST. ANDREW *and
the scallop-shell of pilgrimage.*

ARMS COMMEMORATING THE INTRODUCTION OF CHRISTIANITY

commemorates Offa, who founded the Abbey (now the Cathedral) in expiation of the murder of St. Ethelbert, King of the East Anglians.

Offa's cross (Fig. 36), derived from a coin, denoted the 59th (North Midland) Division during the First World War.

The Coming of the Cross.

Bede tells us that when St. Augustine and his monks first came before King Ethelbert in Thanet, in 596, they bore a silver cross as their banner.

This seems to have been in the minds of the heralds who, centuries later, assigned to Augustine arms consisting of a black shield (suggesting the robe of the Benedictine Order to which he belonged) with a silver cross, and in the first quarter his pallium and archiepiscopal cross, and in the second a silver lily, emblem of the Virgin (Fig. 37).

From this shield the Province of Canterbury selected the pall and cross, and bears them, on a blue shield, to commemorate the man who came to revive the embers of Christianity in southern England, by whose labours the ancient city received the title in her motto, *Ave Mater Angliæ* (Fig. 38).

The dedications and heraldry of three of the earliest English churches recall St. Augustine's personal loyalties. As a Roman he specially reverenced St. Peter and St. Paul, and he also held in high regard St. Andrew, in whose monastery at Rome he had served.

Westminster Abbey, dedicated to St. Peter, flies on occasions a red banner displaying two crossed keys, symbolic of his celestial office. (The Abbey shield, however, commemorates Edward the Confessor.)

St. Paul's emblem, the sword of his martyrdom, stands in the arms of the diocese of London—two crossed swords, gold upon red (Fig. 39) —and also in the shield of the City of London, where it is borne, red on white, with the cross of St. George (Fig. 40). St. Peter and St. Paul were " roughly engraven " (says Stow) on the old seal of the City.

The tradition that the weapon in the City arms is the dagger with which Sir William Walworth slew Wat Tyler is false. Representations of the arms containing the sword exist from a date slightly preceding Wat's death.   As early as 1598, Stow, in his *Survey of London*, emphatically contradicted this persistent legend.   " The armes of this citty," he wrote, " to witte, argent, a playne crosse gules, a sword of St. Paul in the first quarter, and no dagger of W. Walworth, as is fabuled."

Third of the churches recalling Augustine's loyalties is Rochester Cathedral, dedicated to St. Andrew, and displaying his saltire cross, red upon silver, with a golden scallop shell for pilgrimage (Fig. 41).

The establishment of Christianity in the north of England is commemorated by the arms of the See of Durham—a gold cross and four silver lions upon blue.   These are clearly based upon the shield assigned to the Saint-King Oswald (605–642), who is reputed to have founded the See (Fig. 42).   Bede tells us that the cross was raised by Oswald before his great battle with the British King Cadwalla.   The heralds who devised the arms probably included the lions because they had already given a lion to Deira, the southern part of the North-umbrian kingdom, while the number of lions was perhaps suggested by this passage from Bede : " He (Oswald) brought under his dominion all the nations and provinces of Britain, which are divided into four languages, namely, the Britons, the Picts, the Scots and the English."

King Oswald's death at Maserfield, Shropshire, in the battle against Penda of Mercia, is recalled by the arms and name of neighbour-ing Oswestry—a cross and four lions of gold on red.   This shield was borne by a monastery to Oswald's memory founded near the battle-field, and was inherited by the town which grew up near by. Oswestry's seal shows Oswald holding in his right hand a sword, and with his left grasping a tree, the latter emblem expressing phonetically, but with disregard for etymology, the last syllable of the name (*tre*, a place or dwelling).

The Raven.

The history of England during the seventh and eighth centuries is one of conflict between those who bore, or are supposed to have borne, the emblems above noticed, ending in the victory of the golden dragon of Wessex in the hands of Egbert, the ancestor of every sub-

From a coin of Olaf Quaran.

FIG. 43.—THE DANISH RAVEN.

sequent King of England except Cnut, the two Harolds and William the Conqueror.

But scarcely had the golden dragon asserted its supremacy than it was challenged by the Danish raven (Fig. 43). Like the white horse of Kent, this emblem sprang from All-Father Odin, whose wisdom was derived from two ravens, Mind and Memory.

The Danish raven is to-day the crest of Lerwick, capital of the Shetlands, peopled by Vikings whose descendants still celebrate old Norse festivals. The golden shield of the town contains a green dragon-ship, and above it a silver battle-axe in a red chief.

To the Scandinavian peoples the raven was a bird of omen.

" There came two ravens flying which croaked loudly," (sang a Norse poet), " and now, thought the Earl, the blood offering has been accepted, and he thought good luck would be with him any day he liked to go to battle."

Throughout the Sagas ravens were associated with the carnage of battle. Here they are in poetic but gruesome guise :

" The ill-shaped Saxon corpses lay
Heaped up, *the witch-wife's horses'* prey.
She rides by night. At pools of blood
Her horses slake their thirst." . . .

In his Life of Alfred, Asser gives us the following account of the

FIG. 44.—BERMONDSEY.

FIG. 45.—WESTMINSTER ABBEY
AND SCHOOL.

Danish raven standard :—In 878 Danish invaders of Devon were overcome by the English, who

> " gained a very large booty ; and amongst other things the standard called Raven ; for they say that the three sisters of Hingwar and Hubba, daughters of Lodobroch, wove that flag and got it ready in one day.   They say, moreover, that in every battle, wherever that flag went before them, if they were to gain the victory a live crow would appear flying in the middle of the flag ; but if they were doomed to be defeated it would hang down motionless, and this was often proved to be so."

A black Viking ship as the crest of Fulham records the event entered in the Anglo-Saxon Chronicle under the year 879 :

> " The same year assembled a band of pirates, and sat at Fulham by the Thames."

The crest of Wandsworth, too, is a black dragon ship with a silver wyvern on its blue sail.

The Norwegian King Olaf, who assisted Ethelred in his wars against the Danes, is commemorated by the battle-axe, its hilt encircled by a crown, which appears with other emblems in the arms of Bermondsey (Fig. 44).   Here in Tooley Street stood until recently one of the few English churches dedicated to St. Olaf; and the warrior-saint deserves to be remembered by Bermondsey not only on account of the old church, but also because it was at this point on the Thames that he performed the famous exploit which children still tell in the words of an ancient minstrel :

> " London Bridge is broken down—
> Gold is won, and bright renown."

Bermondsey's battle-axe and crown therefore commemorate Olaf's mastery of the Thames by the destruction of the old fortified bridge and the storming of the Danish camp at Southwark. These emblems form the badge of St. Olave's School.

The white horse cut in the chalk near Ashdown and popularly supposed to commemorate the defeat of the Danes by Alfred and Ethelred in 871 actually dates from much earlier than Saxon times.

Edward the Confessor.

Everybody who is familiar with Westminster Abbey must have seen the arms of Edward the Confessor which stand in many places in his greatest monument. They consist of a golden cross " flory " and five gold doves on a blue shield (Fig. 47).

The thirteenth-century heralds who devised this beautiful shield

FIG. 46.—COIN OF EDWARD THE CONFESSOR.

FIG. 47.—ARMS OF EDWARD THE CONFESSOR, *from Westminster Abbey.*

D

based it on a coin of the Confessor, containing the cross usual to the reverse of English money, but in the quarters four doves instead of the customary pellets (Fig. 46). A dove surmounts the sceptre in Edward's seal, and it is clear that he regarded this bird, emblem of piety and gentleness, as his special symbol.

Though posthumously conferred, Edward's arms are of some importance on account of their mediæval and modern associations. They have been incorporated in the arms of Westminster Abbey, School (Fig. 45) and City (Fig. 131); of the old royal borough of Eye in Suffolk, and the West Suffolk County Council; and they are even found in Canada, where they appear in the shield of the See of New Westminster. They were adopted by the Abbey of Dunfermline, founded by the Confessor's great-niece, who became the wife of Malcolm Canmore.

To some of Edward's royal predecessors the heralds assigned modifications of his arms—a gold cross with only four doves for the kings from Edgar onwards, and the cross flory alone for some of the earlier kings, including Alfred. University College, Oxford, which in its optimistic moments claims Alfred as its founder, departs from heraldic tradition by using as arms the cross and four doves attributed to Alfred's successors.

The presence of Edward's arms in the roof of Westminster Hall is a memorial not directly to the Confessor but to Richard II, rebuilder of the hall, who showed such respect for Edward as to bear his banner in battle and marshal his arms on the royal shield.

Another emblem attributed to the Confessor is a hand grasping a ring—the ring he gave as alms to an old pilgrim at the consecration of St. John's Church at the place subsequently called Havering, Essex. The pilgrim was St. John himself, who later sent the ring back to King Edward, with word that he should

"dispose of his goods, for within six months he shall be in the joy of Heaven with me, when he shall have his reward for his chastity and good living."

In allusion to this legend, the Confessor's ring appears in the arms of the Borough of Romford, which embraces Havering.

| *Norman banner and shield.* | *William's standard-bearer with the Papal banner.* | *The Wessex dragon standard.* | *Typical Saxon shields.* |

FIG. 48.—GROUPS FROM THE BAYEUX TAPESTRY.

IV

HASTINGS AND THE CONQUEST

" The German dragon shall hardly get to his holes . . . for a people in wood and in iron coats shall come and revenge upon him his wickedness. They shall restore the ancient inhabitants to their dwellings, and there shall be an open destruction of foreigners. . . . After this shall succeed two dragons, whereof one shall be killed by the arrow of envy, but the other shall return under the shadow of a name. Then shall succeed the Lion of Justice, at whose roar the Gallican towers and the island dragons shall tremble."—Geoffrey of Monmouth, *Prophecies of Merlin.*

WHEN Duke William wrested England from King Harold, heraldry, even in the more advanced countries of Europe, had not flowered. The Bayeux Tapestry, the famous pictorial record of the Norman invasion, shows decorated shields and banners, and attempts have been made to identify individuals thereby, but without very convincing results.

35

Yet Wace, writing in the reign of Henry II, stated :

> " They (the Normans) had shields on their necks and lances in their hands, and all had made cognisances that one Norman might know another by, and that none others bore, so that no Frenchman might perish by the hand of another, and no Frenchman might kill another."

Wace can scarcely have meant that the Normans bore *individual* cognisances, but that there were one or two emblems in use throughout the host to distinguish William's followers as a whole from the Saxons.

This identification of all the members of an army by a distinctive figure was no new thing. We read in St. Olaf's Saga that at the battle of Niesse, half a century before Hastings,

> " the most of his men had white shields, on which the Holy Cross was gilt ; but some had painted it in blue or red."

The reason for this clearly appears in the account of Olaf's last battle, in 1030, when the King ordered :

> " We will have all our men distinguished by a mark, so as to be a field token upon their helmets and shields, by painting the Holy Cross thereupon with white colour. When we come into battle we shall all have one counter-sign and field-cry, ' Forward, forward, Christ-men ! Cross-men ! King's men ! ' "

The King himself had " a white shield on which the Holy Cross was inlaid in gold."

So we may assume that at Hastings the devices on the Norman shields, if they were anything more than merely decorative, had a partisan rather than a personal significance. The Bayeux Tapestry shows us that a dragon was a favourite figure on the Norman shields (Fig. 48). But the dragon was clearly the *English* emblem. It was around the banner of the Golden Dragon of Wessex (Fig. 48)—the " German dragon " of the so-called prophecy quoted at the head of this chapter—that Harold's hus-carles made their last stand. Why should the Normans display their enemies' emblem ?

William claimed to be King of the English by right, and the

prevalence of the dragon on the shields of his followers suggests that he may have deliberately adopted the emblem of the English as an expression of his claim to be their lawful king.

That the Norman Duke had the sanction of the Church for his expedition is shown heraldically by the banner depicted in the Tapestry—a red (or gold) cross on a white ground with a blue border (Fig. 48). This was the flag which received the blessing of Pope Alexander. We may take it as a reminder that William was by no means the submissive son of the Church the Pope hoped to find him, for in later years he answered Pope Gregory's pretensions in these words: " Fealty I never willed to do, nor do I will to do it now. I have never promised it, nor do I find that my predecessors did it to yours."

Upon another Norman banner represented in the Tapestry is a bird which may have been the famous raven of the Norsemen (Fig. 48). This emblem recalls the descent of the Normans from the fierce and adventurous Scandinavian people who harried the shores of England and established themselves firmly in Northern France during the " dark ages " after the fall of Charlemagne's Empire. It suggests that the Normans were not forgetful of their origin, and emphasises the fact that the Anglo-Saxon kingdom finally fell not to a new and unexpected foe, but to a branch of that race which had for generations sought to conquer it.

It has been suggested that the raven in the arms of the family of Corby was derived from the Norse raven on the banner of an ancestor of the family; the name *may* have been derived from the emblem, but more probably the *corbeau* was adopted in reference to the name.

Hastings Fables.

An armed knight holding a red banner containing two golden lions (the traditional arms of the Conqueror) supported the shield of Lord Delaval, and represented Guido de la Val, said to have been a cousin of Duke William and to have borne his head banners at Hastings. Unfortunately Guido is unhistorical.

Other families which, in the face of scathing criticisms by modern genealogists, cling to the legend of an ancestor who fought at Hastings, seek to support their claim by a liberal interpretation of the bearings in their arms. A branch of the St. Johns who display three wagon-horses' collars profess to be descended from the master of William's baggage-wagons; and the Ferrers family seek the origin of their name, and the horseshoes in their shield (Fig. 1), in the office of chief farrier to the Norman army.[1]

A romantic story of Hastings attaches to the name Fortescue. Richard le Fort, it is storied, flung his shield before Duke William at a critical moment in the battle, thereby saving him from death. For this service Fort received the addition of *escue* to his name, and to this day the Fortescues bear the punning motto, *Forte scutum salus ducum*—" A strong shield is the leader's safeguard." A badge of the family is a shield bearing the word Fort.

The anxiety of families to establish a Norman ancestor has been responsible for many such fables, and as a corrective nothing could be better than this quotation from the late Mr. Fox-Davies's *Armorial Families*.

> " If any ordinary individual tell you he is descended in the male line from someone who figures upon the glorious roll of Battle Abbey, or that his ancestor ' came over with the Conqueror,' write him down a perverter of the truth at once."

On the other hand, there are families who despise the upstart Norman stock. The Pilkingtons, for instance, claim to have been a notable family in England before the Conquest, and point to their crest of a husbandman as evidence of an ancestor who disguised himself as a thresher to escape from the Norman soldiery after Hastings.

[1] It is much more probable that they were originally *de Ferrieres*, a place-name. Here an old custom of heraldic note may be recalled. In the words of Camden, " every baron of the realm, the first time he comes through the town of Okeham where the Ferrers seat was, shall give a horseshoe to nail on the Castle gate. If he refuse, the bailiff of the manor has power to stop his coach and take one off the horses' feet. But mainly they give five, ten or twenty shillings, more or less, as they please, and in proportion to the gift the shoe is made larger or smaller, with the name and title of the donor cut upon it. So it is nailed upon the gate." The collection of horse-shoes may still be seen.

FIG. 49.—LAMBETH, *embodying the chequers of the Warrennes, Earls of Surrey ; the mitre and crozier of the Archbishop of Canterbury ; and the golden roundels of the Duchy of Cornwall.*

The Conquest.

The piecemeal nature of the true Conquest which followed Hastings is curiously suggested by the similarity between the arms of certain cities and towns in widely separated parts of the country. For instance, the gold and blue chequers of the Warrennes, Earls of Surrey (Fig. 2), appear in the shields of places ranging from Lewes to Dewsbury and including Lambeth (Fig. 49) This indicates not only the extent of the possessions granted by the Duke to William de Warrenne, ancestor of the chequers-bearing family, but also the scattered nature of their territory, and indirectly the manner in which Duke William distributed the spoils of conquest. Faced with a clamorous demand for land by a host of adventurers, he parcelled out the country as he won it, granting first territorial hors-d'œuvres promissory of the feast to come, and later serving more substantial courses. The fortunate but not necessarily premeditated result of this enforced policy was that the Duke prevented his followers obtaining large tracts of land in one district, and setting themselves up as serious rivals to the monarch.

Only in the key-counties on the borders of his realm—Durham, Chester, Shropshire and Kent—did William permit great semi-independent jurisdictions to arise. The mitre of the See of Durham, plumed like a helmet and with a coronet about its rim (Fig. 42), is symbolic of the palatinate jurisdiction which William conferred upon that bishopric, the patrimony of St. Cuthbert, which " lay as a sacred boundary between England and Scotland." The seal of Lord Crewe, a seventeenth-century Bishop of Durham, contained the figure of a fully-armed man on horseback, his warlike appearance being palliated by an inscription suggesting his arms to be of a spiritual nature : *Propterea accipite armaturam Dei et galeam salutis assumite et gladium spiritus*. But the seal clearly referred to the soldierly character of the old-time bishops. The Palatinate was transferred to the Crown in 1836, but the Bishop of Durham still retains the coronet about his mitre.

The presence of two gold lions on red (the supposed arms of the Conqueror) in the shield of the See of Lincoln commemorates the ecclesiastical reorganisation undertaken by William and Lanfranc, which resulted in the transfer of the centre of the vast northern bishopric from Dorchester-on-Thames to Lincoln.

Pevensey, which was granted to Gilbert de Aquila and came to be known as the Honour of the Eagle, still uses as arms a red eagle upon gold in allusion to the Norman family.

The Survival of the Dragon.

What became of the golden dragon which was overthrown at Hastings, yet was also victorious there if we are right in thinking that William adopted it, even before he seized the kingdom?

In the passage at the head of this chapter, Geoffrey of Monmouth refers in heraldic terms to the combatants at Hastings, and to the subsequent kings of the English. Of the two dragons who follow the overthrow of the German dragon (the English standard) the first is clearly William Rufus, " killed by the arrow of envy," and the second is presumably Stephen. The Lion of Justice, as will be seen in the following chapter, is Henry I. Geoffrey was true to heraldry in attributing a dragon to the Saxons and a lion to Henry, and he was probably equally correct in speaking of the first Norman kings as dragons.

Historically, the dragon is more properly regarded as William I's emblem than the two lions posthumously conferred on him by the heralds.

We have certain evidence that the Dragon standard was used by four of William's successors, namely, Richard I, Henry III, Edward I and Henry V.   In his account of Richard's crusade, Richard of Devizes wrote : " The terrible standard of the dragon is borne in front unfurled."   Henry III is recorded as having issued a mandate " to cause a dragon to be made in fashion of a standard of red silk sparkling all over with gold, the tongue of which should be made to resemble burning fire and appear to be continually moving, the eyes of sapphires or other suitable stones."   It is recorded that at Crécy King Edward raised " his unconquered standard of the Dragon Gules," and that it made its appearance again at Agincourt.

So this ancient and vigorous monster, descended from an ensign of Imperial Rome, continued as our national standard until the fifteenth century, and is to this day a princely emblem in our land.

We may here notice parenthetically that the so-called griffins which support the shield of the City of London (one of which commands Fleet-street) are in reality dragons, your griffin being an eagle as to his upper parts and netherly a lion.   But the London dragons are not related to the old national emblem.   They had an accidental and unnatural origin.   Over the shield in a sixteenth-century seal of the City is a helmet with a fan-shaped metal crest, painted with a red cross as in the arms.   In the following century the City fathers seem to have imagined that this metal fan was the wing of a monster, and, as anatomists reconstruct an extinct animal from one small bone, they created the dragon to which this supposed wing belonged, and set him up to guard and support their shield.   So the City dragons have no heraldic ancestry.   In the time of Richard II the shield in the civic seal was supported by lions.

Rufus and the English.

The preservation of the dragon was in accordance with the Norman kings' policy of placating their English subjects by identifying the crown with what national sentiment existed. In this connection a device attributed to William Rufus by the seventeenth-century herald, Guillim, may have some historical significance.

" It is storied," wrote Guillim, " that the old eagles make a proof of their young by exposing them to the Sun-beames, and such as cannot steadily behold their brightness are cast forth as unworthy to be acknowledged their Off-spring. In which respect *William Rufus*, King of this Land, gave for his device an Eagle, looking against the sun, with this word, *Perferro*, I can endure it, to signify he was no whit degenerate from his puissant Father the Conqueror."

The Norman baronage would have been better pleased if William II had indeed proved himself to be degenerate ; in fact, there was a strong movement to place the Conqueror's eldest son, the weak and careless Robert, upon the English throne. It was not to them, therefore, that William's device was intended to appeal, but rather to the English ; and it appears to have been less a personal cognisance than a political cartoon, invented to suggest to his English subjects that Rufus rather than Robert was the man to protect their interests against the barons. Certain it is that at the outset of his reign William threw himself upon the loyalty of the English, who mustered in strength to expel the rebel lords, doubtless feeling that however oppressive the royal hand it must be less objectionable than baronial anarchy.

Henry I seems to have been the first English king actually to display the lion, though, as we have noted, two lions are regarded as having been the arms of the first two Williams. The lions of England are the subject of the following chapter.

Stephen.

To Stephen of Blois, more knight than king, is attributed the badge of a sagittary, or centaur armed with bow and arrow, and it has been conjectured that this emblem commemorated a victory won by his archers. An alternative theory is that he took this badge from the zodiacal sign under which his reign began.

Another badge said to have been used by Stephen was a plume of three ostrich feathers, with the motto, *Vi nulla invertitur ordo*, " By

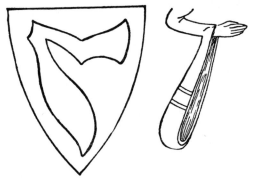

FIGS. 50 AND 51.—HASTINGS:
The " maunch " and its origin.

FIG. 52.—DE QUINCEY:
A design probably based on armour.

no force is their form altered." This must not be connected with the " Prince of Wales's feathers," which had a different origin.

The Kentish family of Dering point to the three red roundels above the blue fesse in their silver shield as a memorial of the battle of Lincoln where Stephen was taken prisoner. Normannus Fitz Dering, who made gallant efforts to rescue the King, was found dead after the battle with his shield covered with blood, whence, it is said, the red roundels borne by his descendants. The crest of the family, a black horse, refers to their claim to have been notable people in the old Saxon kingdom of Kent.

Fashions of the Times.

Two coats of arms give us a glimpse of the styles of costume and armour during the twelfth century.

The first is that of the Hastings family, gold with a red " maunch " —a lady's sleeve with a long baggy cuff (Figs. 50 and 51). " William de Hastings, the founder of the family, was Steward of the Household to Henry I, in whose reign the illuminations in which we discover this curiously shaped sleeve were, it is most probable, executed " (Planché, *British Costume*).

Possibly Hastings adopted this emblem in token of some lady's favour. A more interesting point for the herald is that in the Hastings shield we have an emblem which seems to have been in continuous use since the reign of Henry I, and is therefore an unusually early example of a personal cognisance which became hereditary.

The second hint at old fashions is the shield of De Quincey, Earl of Winchester—red with seven gold " mascles " (Fig. 52). This device was probably suggested by the armour of the period, which consisted of lozenge-shaped pieces of steel superimposed on leather.

To digress for a moment on the subject of shields illustrating armour, a more famous and later instance is that of the Isle of Man —the three mailed legs, bent at the knee and joined at the thigh, on red (Fig. 53). " The arms of Man are legs," is a well-known heraldic paradox. Imagine this shield set in the geographical position of the Isle, and you will appreciate the saying : " The Isle of Man kneels to England, kicks at Scotland, and spurns Ireland."

FIG. 53.—ISLE OF MAN.

Fig. 54.—*Early Heraldic Lion.*   Fig. 55.—*Two Lions are*   Fig. 56.—*Three Lions were*
attributed to Henry II.   *adopted by* Richard I.

V

THE LIONS OF ENGLAND

" The *Lion* (saith *Farnesius*) is a lively *Image* of a good *Souldier*, who must be *valiant* of *courage, strong* of *body, politicke* in *counsell*, and a *foe* to *feare*."—Guillim, *Display of Heraldry.*

" THREE leopards of fine gold set on red; courant, fierce, haughty and cruel; to signify that like them the King is dreadful to his enemies, for his bite is slight to none who brave his anger; and yet towards such as seek his friendship or submit to his power his kindness is soon rekindled." Thus the armorial Roll of Caerlaverock (1300) describes the arms of the King of England.

Three lions (for in ancient heraldry a leopard was but a prowling lion) have stood in the Royal Arms of England since the reign of Richard I. Their origin is uncertain, but is the subject of an interesting though doubtful theory.

The Lion of Justice.

The seals of the first and second Williams and Henry I are bare of heraldry, but Henry seems to have used a single lion as a badge, and Planché thinks this may have been in allusion to the title " Lion of Justice " by which Geoffrey of Monmouth, in the prophecies of Merlin previously quoted, refers to the King.

45

FIG. 57.—GEOFFREY OF ANJOU,
*with the shield given him by
Henry I, his father-in-law.*

FIG. 58.—THE LIONS OF ENGLAND,
*from tiles in the Chapter House at
Westminster.*

If so, in the light of history we may regard the first of our English lions as commemorating the foundation of the administrative and legal system by the organisation of the *curia regis* for financial and judicial business, the establishment of itinerant justices to carry the King's law throughout the realm, and the strengthening of the popular courts of shire and hundred to resist the encroachment of feudal franchises.

For lack of contemporary illustration the drawing of a single lion for Henry I is taken from examples of a rather later date in Rochester Cathedral (Fig. 54).

It is significant that it was in the reign of Henry I that the first lion was seen in England, in the King's menagerie at Woodstock.

Our chief reason for believing that the lion was Henry I's peculiar emblem is its prevalence in the heraldry of the King's descendants and those connected by marriage with his family.

When Henry knighted his son-in-law, Geoffrey, Count of Anjou (father of Henry II), he gave him a shield charged with little golden lions, and this appears on an enamelled figure of the Count formerly on his tomb (Fig. 57). Here he has also a lion on his cap, the forerunner of the English royal crest.

Geoffrey's grandson, William Longuespée, Earl of Salisbury (son of Henry II by Fair Rosamund), bore similar arms, placing his golden lions upon a blue shield. With the evidence that Henry II himself bore two lions we shall deal below.

Henry I's descendants through his illegitimate children all bore one or more lions in various attitudes and with or without other emblems, and from this evidence we deduce the probability that the lion was the badge of Henry I, though we have no contemporary representation of such a device (see Table I).

The Second Lion.

Whence, then, came the second lion of England? It has been suggested that it came into the arms through Henry I's marriage with Adeliza, daughter of Godfrey of Louvain, who bore a lion (thinks Planché) in allusion to his name (Leuwon: Leones). But there is

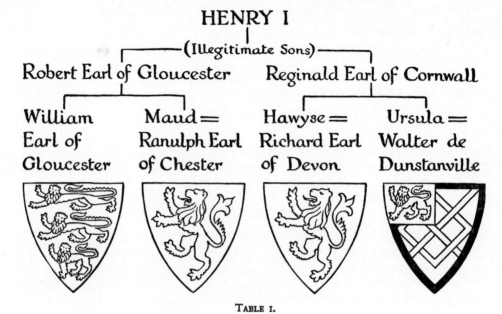

TABLE I.

no proof that the second lion was intended to denote this match. It
may have been added merely for artistic effect.

Thus from his grandfather Henry II is supposed to have inherited
two gold lions on red, but they first appear as an undoubted shield
of arms in the seal of his son, John. But Prince John's lions looked
not out of the shield but over their shoulders (*reguardant*). This
may have been deliberate, to distinguish the son's arms from the
father's. Two lions differently placed were probably used by Henry's
elder son, Richard I, during his crusade (Chapter VI).

In the course of time the two lions came to be regarded as having
been the arms of all English kings from William I to Henry II, and
they appear in the shields of several foundations connected with
those monarchs. They are quartered in the shield of the Duchy of
Brunswick, owing to the marriage of Maud, daughter of Henry II,
to Henry V, Duke of Bavaria. When Maud's remote descendant,
George, Duke of Brunswick and Luneberg, ascended the English
throne as George I, the two lions were reintroduced into our Royal
Arms and remained there for a century.

The Third Lion.

Just as Henry I is supposed to have acquired the second lion through his marriage, so it is thought Henry II added the third when he married Eleanor of Aquitaine, whose arms are known to have been a single golden lion on red. The three lions as we know them (Figs. 56 and 58) were first used by Richard I, being placed on his seal in 1194.

The Lions in Civic Heraldry.

Many English cities and towns bear in their arms one or more of the royal lions. Canterbury has one on its red chief above the three

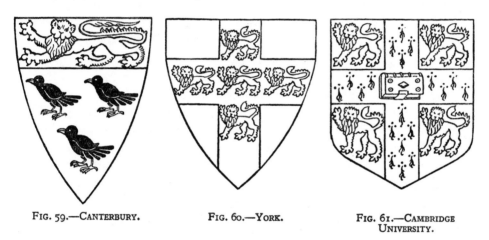

FIG. 59.—CANTERBURY.   FIG. 60.—YORK.   FIG. 61.—CAMBRIDGE UNIVERSITY.

Cornish choughs of St. Thomas-a-Becket (Fig. 59). York has five on a cross of St. George (Fig. 60). Winchester has two supporting the middle one of five silver castles on red. Cambridge University has four lions on red about its ermine cross bearing a red-bound book (Fig. 61). The three lions also form the arms of the Channel Islands.

The Planta Genista.

From his father, Henry II inherited the famous badge which gave the Plantagenets their name (Fig. 62). The broom plant, or *planta genista*, " in early summer makes the open country of Anjou

E

and Maine a blaze of living gold," and it is natural that the Counts of Anjou should have adopted as a badge so familiar a feature of their lands.

Count Geoffrey appears to have been the first to wear the plant—we are told that he usually had a sprig of it in his cap.

The broom-cod badge was used by Richard I, and also by John and Henry III, despite John's loss of the lands whence it came. After an apparent lapse during the reigns of the three Edwards, its use was revived by Richard II and Henry IV, and was continued intermittently by other members of the Royal Family down to the reign of Elizabeth, who had a costume embroidered with *planta genista*.

As the badge gave rise to the name Plantagenet, so the name reacted upon the badge, and a genet, a kind of cat common in the south of France, was placed between the broom-cods by Henry IV the better to express the latter part of the name.

The pride with which the Angevins regarded their badge is suggested by Maurice Hewlett in *Richard Yea-and-Nay*. Richard addresses his little son, born to him in the Holy Land by Jehane of St. Pol, thus : " When I lay, even as thou, Fulke, naked by my mother, my father sent for a branch of the broom and stuck it in the pillow against I could carry it. And shalt thou be without, boy? Art thou not of the broom-bearers? " And he sent the Bishop of Salisbury straightway " to the moor of Angers. Pluck me a branch of the wild broom and return."

The *planta genista* appears in the arms of some English towns.

Henry II is also credited with the badge of an eagle—perhaps the Imperial eagle inherited from his mother, the Empress Maud, widow of the Emperor Henry IV. Camden tells us that the King had the eagle painted in his great chamber at Winchester, " with four young chickens, whereof three pecked and scratched him, the fourth picked at his eyes." To those who asked the meaning he replied, " that they were his sons which did so peck him, and that John, the youngest, whom he loved best, practised his death more busily than the rest."

FIG. 62.—FIRST GREAT SEAL OF RICHARD I,
showing crusading emblems, planta genista, and royal lion.

VI

THE CRUSADES

"Then might you have seen many a banner and pennon of various forms floating in the breeze . . . helmets with crests, brilliant with jewels, and shining mails, and shields, emblazoned with lions, or flying dragons in gold."—Geoffrey de Vinsauf, *Itinerary of Richard I.*

ALTHOUGH we can trace the beginnings of heraldry (as distinct from mere decoration) to a period before King Richard's crusade, it was during that great adventure that the need for a developed system of armory became apparent, and the heraldic emblems and nomenclature of the Middle Ages bear many traces of impressions left by the later Holy Wars.

The impetus which Richard's expedition gave to heraldry is seen when a comparison is made between the arms in use before the Crusade and those in the Roll of Arms compiled in the reign of Henry III. There is a certain sameness in twelfth-century armorials, due largely to the frequent use of a few charges, which were variously grouped and coloured to produce different arms. The heraldic

51

" ordinaries " (described in Chapter I), a few of the best known beasts and birds, and common objects with a punning reference to particular surnames were the whole of the herald's stock-in-trade.

But the Crusades gave birth to many new heraldic figures. The enrichment of heraldry at this time is typical of the manner in which the ideas of Western Europe in art, science and philosophy were widened by contact with the more ancient culture of the East.

The Cross.

Foremost among the emblems of the Holy Wars was, of course, the cross (Fig. 63). Like Spenser's knight, every man of the Christian armies :

> " Upon his breast a bloody Cross he bore,
> The dear remembrance of his dying Lord,
> For whose sweete sake that glorious badge he wore,
> And dead, as living, ever Him ador'd ;
> Upon his shield the like was also scor'd."

Pope Urban II, the preacher of the First Crusade, decreed this practice at the Council of Clermont in 1095. " The Cross of Christ," he told the crusaders, " is the symbol of your salvation. Wear it, a red, a bloody cross, on your breasts and shoulders, as a token that His help will never fail you ; as the pledge of a vow which can never be recalled."

His words echoed those of St. Olaf, who sixty years before had ordered his men to paint the Holy Cross on their shields before their encounter with the pagan forces of Scandinavia.

The colour of the cross was later varied to distinguish the soldiers of one country from those of another. In the Third Crusade the red cross was appropriated by the French, while the English displayed white crosses, and the Flemings green. But when the English adopted St. George as their patron saint they made his red cross their own, and in this ancient crusading device we see the beginnings of our national flag, the Union Jack.

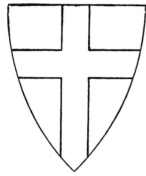 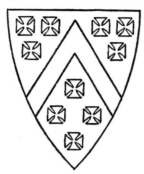 

FIG. 63.—THE CROSS.   FIG. 64.—BERKELEY.   FIG. 65.—THE " MALTESE "
                                                 CROSS.

Edward III, when he founded the Order of the Garter under the patronage of St. George,

> " appoynted his Souldiers to wear white Coats or Jackets, with a red Crosse before and behinde over their Armour, . . ." and " . . . it was not only a comely but a stately sight to behold the English Battles, like the rising Sunne, to glitter farre off in that pure hew; when the Souldiers of other Nations in their baser weedes could not be discerned " (Speed).

So for many years the red cross remained the uniform of English armies, and even after its disuse our soldiers continued to wear its martial red until the exigencies of warfare compelled them to don " baser weedes " which " could not be discerned."

When Richard II invaded Scotland in 1386 he commanded that every man who followed him should bear " a sign of the arms of St. George, large, bothe before and behynde," lest he be slain in default thereof by his own party; " and that non enemy do bere the same token or crosse of St. George, notwithstanding if he be prisoner upon payne of deth."

(The red cross of the Royal Army Medical Corps is not the cross of St. George, but was formed by reversing the arms of Switzerland—a white cross upon red—because it was at the Convention of Geneva in 1864 that special protection was ensured for the sick and wounded and those tending them.)

Certain families which have crosses in their shields claim that they signify some ancestor's participation in a crusade. Camden tells us that "the Lord Barkleys, who bare first Gules a Chevron Argent, after one of them had taken upon him the Cross, . . . to serve in those wars, inserted ten Crosses 'paty' in his shield" (Fig. 64).

Several of the crusading military orders adopted an eight-pointed cross (Fig. 65), each point being supposed to stand for one of the Beatitudes. The Templars bore the cross red on white, the Hospitallers white on black. The Hospitallers' cross is still the badge of the Order of St. John of Jerusalem, which assigns significance to each of the points, namely, Observation, Tact, Resource, Dexterity, Explicitness, Discrimination, Perseverance and Sympathy—essential qualities in ambulance and hospital work. The eight-pointed cross (or "Maltese cross," from its association with the Knights of Malta) is found, with various embellishments, in the insignia of the Royal Victorian Order, the military classes of the Order of the Bath, and several foreign orders of chivalry.

While we have been mainly concerned with the mediæval and modern associations of the cross, our story would be incomplete without reference to its pre-Christian significance. Latter-day criticism, while prepared to admit the probable existence of a Christian soldier named Giorgios, points out that, like other saints, he has become heir-at-legend to several personages of pagan mythology. His traditional contest with the dragon identifies him with a common figure in Aryan stories; he is, in fact, none other than the Sun-champion destroying the powers of darkness. He is Tammuz and Adonis, Baal and Osiris, Mithras and Apollo. His red cross is the fiery cross of the ancient sun-cults; and while it has for us a higher meaning than it had for our pre-Christian ancestors, we may hold it in the greater reverence because through many ages it has symbolised man's perception of the Deity within the measure of his understanding. Such is the central figure of our national flag.

Arms of Jerusalem.

Probably no arms have been more reverently regarded than those of the crusaders' Kingdom of Jerusalem, which consisted of five

FIG. 66.—JERUSALEM. FIG. 67.—LICHFIELD. FIG. 68.—ISLINGTON.

crosses (Fig. 66). The central one is a large cross " potent," or crutch-shaped, and it stands between four small plain crosses. All the crosses are of gold upon a silver shield. This violates the well-known heraldic rule that metal may not be placed upon metal, and it is supposed that the violation was intentional in view of the special sacredness of the arms.

Various explanations have been offered as to the meaning of these arms. One writer sees in the form of the central cross a combination of the letters I and H, standing for Iesus and Hierusalem; but this idea vanishes in face of some early representations of the shield in which the arms of the cross terminate not in rectangular pieces but in small knobs. The number of crosses has been thought to refer to the Five Wounds of Christ; but the most probable theory is that the crosses symbolise the Saviour and the Four Evangelists.

As to the execution of the arms in the two precious metals, there is a suggestion that the Psalmist's reference to Jerusalem may have influenced the heralds: " Though ye have lien among the pots, yet shall ye be as the wings of a dove covered with silver, and her feathers with yellow gold." To modern minds this explanation may seem to be somewhat fantastic, but in the Middle Ages much importance was attached to the prophetic interpretation of the Scriptures; and it may well be that the designers of the arms of Jerusalem had this text in mind, and felt they were assisting at its fulfilment.

Between the arms of Jerusalem and those of the See of Lichfield there is a resemblance which cannot be due merely to a coincidence. In the latter shield the central cross is squared at the centre, and the four small crosses are of the form known as " paty " (Fig. 67). The field is divided vertically into red and silver, and the crosses are silver on the red and gold on the silver.

An early Bishop of Lichfield is believed to have assumed these arms after a journey to the Holy City; but as the patron of the Cathedral is St. Chad (seventh-century Bishop of Mercia), the arms have come to be incorrectly associated with him. They were deflected still further from their true significance when they became the basis of the arms of the family of Chad, baronets of eighteenth-century creation.

The arms of Jerusalem are quartered in the shield of Queens' College, Cambridge, founded by Henry VI's queen, the unhappy Margaret of Anjou, daughter of the landless King of Naples and Jerusalem (Fig. 144); and the arms of Lichfield have been embodied in the shields of Selwyn College, Cambridge; Denstone College, Derby School, and other foundations linked in some way with the Diocese.

The Lichfield arms are now generally coloured red and white throughout. This is a pity, for the disappearance of the gold crosses obscures their connection with the arms of the Holy City.

Islington recalls in its arms its ancient association with the crusaders through the Knights of St. John, who once held the manor of Highbury, the gold cross potent on red in the first quarter of the Borough shield (Fig. 68) being taken from that of Jerusalem. Hackney's arms include a quartering divided horizontally black and white (like the Templars' banner) and containing an eight-pointed cross, white on the black half of the ground and red on the white, in token that the Manor was once held by the Templars, and afterwards by the Hospitallers.

The nails of the Cross also figure in early heraldry. The Anstruthers explain their three black piles on silver (Fig. 69) as a conventional representation of Passion nails, Henry, Lord Anstruther, having accompanied St. Louis to the Holy Land.

FIG. 69.—ANSTRUTHER.
*The piles are said to represent
the Nails of the Cross.*

FIG. 70.—CŒUR-DE-LION.
*Presumed arms during the
crusading period of his reign.*

Cœur-de-Lion.

We pass from religious to royal emblems associated with the
wars of the Cross. Our crusader-king, Richard I, was likened by
contemporary writers to a lion. Richard of Devizes said of him
that " he raged like the fiercest lion, and vented his anger in a manner
worthy that noble beast." Such passages as this, as well as his famous
nickname Cœur-de-Lion, have reference to the King's habitual use
of a lion as a badge or banner ; though the name has the usual explana-
tory fable which tells how Richard, being attacked by a lion, tore
out with his hands the royal beast's heart.

The first Great Seal of Richard, used during the crusading period
of his reign, represents him with a single ramping lion on his shield
(Fig. 62). But as the lion faces the centre of the shield, of which
only half is visible, it has been conjectured that there was another
lion on the hidden half, and consequently Richard I has been credited
with the arms of two golden fighting lions upon red (Fig. 70).

This theory has been contested by Mr. Oswald Barron in the
Encyclopædia Britannica, but it is to some extent borne out by Geoffrey
de Vinsauf, the chronicler of Richard's crusade, who, describing the
King's appearance on a certain occasion, states that his saddle " glit-
tered with gold spangles interspersed with red, while on the hinder
part two small lions of gold were turned towards each other with

FIG. 71.—SECOND GREAT SEAL OF RICHARD I,
showing the sun and moon, Royal Arms of three lions, and lion on helmet.

their mouths open, and one pointed to the other with each of the fore-legs as though stretched out to devour."

We have seen how strong is the presumptive evidence that Henry II bore two lions; we know that his son John bore two lions; and the cumulative evidence is in favour of the theory that in the earlier part of his career Richard also bore two lions. The fact that Richard's lions are " rampant-combattant " while John's are " passant-reguardant " supports this view, for the brothers would naturally have borne their paternal lions in different attitudes so that their arms might be distinct.

Richard's chroniclers refer to his lion standard. Sir Bernard Burke seems to have imagined that this was " the banner of the Holy City—the dormant lion of Judah—the badge of David and Solomon." But it is unlikely that the Christian king would have displayed a device associated with the despised Jews. There can be no doubt that Richard's lion standard was personal, and had nothing to do with the Holy City.

On his return from the crusade, Richard adopted the three lions "passant-guardant" which have ever since been the Royal Arms of England, and still hold the premier place in the Queen's shield. Richard embodied these arms in a new Great Seal (Fig. 71), and obtained a considerable sum of money from his subjects by requiring all existing charters to be confirmed under the new seal.

The Sun and the Moon.

Upon Richard's two seals are emblems which merit attention in connection with the Crusades. The first seal contains two crescents, each surmounted by a star-shaped object (Fig. 62). I deliberately avoid describing it as a star because I think it may originally have been intended for the sun, for reasons which follow.

The crescent referred to the King's vocation as a crusader. It was the ancient emblem of Byzantium, connected with its presiding goddess, who had saved the city from a night assault by Philip of Macedon by causing the moon to shine with unexpected brilliance. A popular theory that the badge on Richard's seal represents the Star of Bethlehem in ascendancy over the half-moon of the Infidel is false, for as yet the crescent was not the emblem of the Turks, and to apply the phrase " Cross versus Crescent " to the Crusades is anachronistic.

Describing King Richard's appearance at Cyprus, Geoffrey de Vinsauf tells us, " he was clothed in a vest of rose-coloured stuff ornamented with rows of crescents of solid silver, like orbs of the Sun shining in thick profusion."

On Richard's second seal the moon (now at the full) is accom-

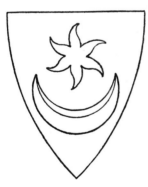

FIG. 72.—PORTSMOUTH.

FIG. 73.—TURKEY.

panied by the sun (Fig. 71), and this inclines me to think that the celestial body above the crescent on the first seal also represents the sun.   This view is supported by Guillim's statement that the sun figured in another of Richard's badges—a sun over two anchors, with the motto, *Christo Duce*, " a worthie and princely choice of so heavenly a Pilote," comments the herald.   And we have also these lines recorded by Speed, as having been written by a contemporary of Richard I :

> *Miro cano ; Sol occubuit,*
> *Nox nulla secuta est.*

Speed translates them :

> " A wonder strange I write,
> The sunne did set, yet was no night.

Meaning that though Henrie were dead, yet the glory and happinesse of the Land was not thereby clouded, for that Richard was another Sunne. . . ."

If the sun was a badge of Richard I, the " sunburst " badge of Edward III and the " sun in splendour " of Richard II may have been revivals of what they knew to have been an old royal emblem.

Speed, however, calls the object above the crescent a star, and quotes a " loftie and Mathematicall " conjecture that it represents the star Cor Leonis, and that Richard's famous nickname was thus derived.   And whatever its origin it is now generally regarded as a star.

This star and crescent badge was used by John and Henry III, who took the cross from reasons of policy but never fulfilled their crusader vows.   It appears on the seal of John de Warrenne, Earl of Surrey (Fig. 2), a constant adherent to Henry III.   It forms the arms of Portsmouth (Fig. 72), which received its first charter from Richard I, and appears in the shield of Dartmouth (Fig. 114) in token that the crusading host set sail from that port.

Seized from the Christians by the Turks in the fifteenth century, the star and crescent badge has ever since remained the Mohammedan emblem.   When it appeared on the medal presented by the Sultan in 1801 to English officers who had taken part in the Egyptian campaign, the descendants of the crusaders received a Christian emblem at the hands of the Infidel.

In 1927, New Turkey devised arms to replace those of the Sultanate. The star and crescent were retained and set upon a red shield above the white wolf of the Turks standing on a lance (Fig. 73). The wolf totem recalls dim ages when the Turks were wandering in a tribal state in Central Asia. Legend tells that a white wolf appeared to guide the people across precipitous mountains to the fertile lands of the West. The arms are intended to point to Turkey's westward career of conquest, and the victorious resurrection of her old national spirit.

Other Crusading Emblems.

Besides the crescent, several other common heraldic charges owe their origin to the Crusades, notably the scallop shell and the water budget, but it does not follow that every family that has such emblems in its arms may boast a crusading ancestor, as these charges passed into general heraldic use, and were adopted by many men whose forefathers did not see the Holy Land.

The " scallop shell of quiet " was an emblem of pilgrimage. Assigned as a badge to St. James, patron of pilgrims, with reference to his original occupation as a fisherman, it was worn by those who made pilgrimage not only to the Holy Land but to the famous shrines in England and other countries. From its use on garments to its appearance in armorial shields was a natural step, and the shell became a familiar heraldic charge at an early date.

A few coats-of-arms which contain scallop shells clearly refer to the Crusades. The family of Villiers have borne a silver shield with a red cross, and thereon five gold shells (Fig. 74), since Sir Richard de Villiers took part in the crusade of Prince Edward. He relinquished his old arms—three white cinquefoils on black, derived from the cinquefoil of his feudal lord, the Earl of Leicester—for this shield combining the emblems of St. George and St. James. A more famous bearer of these arms was Villiers de L'Isle-Adam, last Grand

Master of the Knights of St. John of Rhodes, who led the heroic defence of Rhodes against the forces of Soliman the Magnificent in 1522.

A cross and three scallop shells appear in the arms of John Kendal, Prior of the English Knights of St. John of Jerusalem in 1480 and commander of the cavalry protecting pilgrims against the Turks (Fig. 75).

Three silver scallop shells on red (Fig. 76) were the arms of the family of Dacre, which, according to Dugdale, took their name from

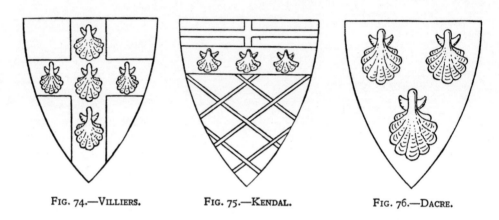

FIG. 74.—VILLIERS.   FIG. 75.—KENDAL.   FIG. 76.—DACRE.

an ancestor who distinguished himself at the siege of Acre. Unfortunately for this story there is no record of any such exploit in contemporary chronicles, and Dacre was an English place-name long before the Third Crusade. However, the arms of Dacre, if not the name, may well be of crusading origin. Sir Walter Scott suggests their legend when he describes Lord Dacre's

" banner tall
That stream'd o'er Acre's conquered wall."

The water budget, a pair of leather bottles borne on a staff over the shoulder, was an article of supreme importance to armies in the parched Eastern lands, and naturally finds a place in crusading heraldry. It appears in the arms of Roos, who derived it from their kinsmen, the Trusbuts; and the three budgets—*trois boutz*—in the shield of the latter family are clearly a pun upon their name (Fig. 77).

The three blue water budgets on gold of the Bourchiers may have denoted some ancestor's part on a crusade, especially as their crest is a Saracen king's head. But here again a pun can be traced, as the family name variously appears as Bucy, Boues and Bouser, suggesting the old word for drink.

The golden roundel, as is natural with so simple a form, is more ancient as an emblem than the Crusades, but the terms " bezant "

 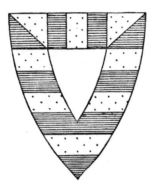 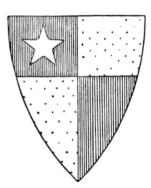

FIG. 77.—TRUSBUTS.   FIG. 78.—MORTIMER.   FIG. 79.—DE VERE.

and " talent " applied to it are of Eastern origin, the former being derived from the name Byzantium, the golden roundel being supposed to represent a Byzantine coin.

The arms of Mortimer are possibly a conventional representation of the Dead Sea, to which the family name clearly refers in its Latinised form, *De Mortuo Mare*. They are indescribable in anything but heraldic language, but picture the illustration (Fig. 78) coloured, the pieces in the border being alternately blue and gold, and the central escutcheon silver, and your imagination may conjure up a vision of the waters of the Dead Sea set amid desert sands under a blue sky.

The arms of De Vere, a shield divided into red and gold quarters with a silver star (Fig. 79), recall a romantic story of the Crusades which may be repeated as an instance of many such fancies. Upon a dark night, a band of Christians were engaged by the Turks, and

"God willing the safety of the Christians showed a white star . . . on the Christian host, which to every man's sight did light and arrest upon the standard of Aubrey de Vere, there shining excessively."

In fact it is probable that the star was introduced by the De Veres to distinguish their arms from others consisting of red and gold quarters.   As we shall see, the same star of the De Vere's was the cause of their defeat at the battle of Barnet during the Wars of the Roses. It appears, with other emblems, in the shield of Kensington, where the De Veres were Lords of the Manor from the Conquest until the beginning of the sixteenth century.

The Saracen's head crest of Dawnay and some other families is an obvious reminiscence of the Holy Wars, but here again the emblem has passed into the regular stock-in-trade of the herald, and does not always denote a crusading ancestor.

Boastful arms of this character are said to have brought Sir Reginald de Chatillon to his death.   Having personally beheaded three captive Saracen chiefs, he depicted their heads in his shield.   Captured by Saladin, his arms proclaimed his exploit too plainly, and he met the fate he had meted out to others.

The Templars.

The arms of the Knights Templars are well known to those who frequent the Inns of Court, where they may be seen carved in stone in several places in the Inner Temple.   The shield now contains a pegasus, but this is a corruption of their original arms, which consisted of two knights riding on one horse.   This is said to commemorate their humble beginnings, when they were so poor that the Master and his friend had but one horse between them, for the Templars were sworn to individual poverty, however wealthy they might become as an Order.   The Templars' badge was an Agnus Dei carrying a banner (Fig. 1), and this on a red cross now forms the arms of the Middle Temple.

The Templars' white and black banner, called Beauseant, hinted that they were " fair and favourable to the friends of Christ, black and terrible to His enemies."

The Heraldic Zoo.

To the fragmentary information gleaned by the crusaders and pilgrims in the course of their Eastern travels we owe some of the remarkable fauna of heraldry. The crocodile probably provided the mediæval dragon with his scaly frightfulness. Rumours of the rhinoceros, confused perhaps with the desert antelopes, produced the unicorn. Sailors, then as now " splendaciously mendacious," passed off the narwhal's horn as that of the unicorn, and when the translators of the Bible used the word " unicorn " to render some untranslatable Hebrew name, they placed the existence of the beast beyond question so far as our devout ancestors were concerned ; and so in due course it found its way into our royal heraldry.

The crusaders also encountered the ostrich, and were greatly impressed with its digestive capacity, wherefore the heralds generally represented it as chewing iron, a horseshoe for preference. Some traveller, too, met a giraffe, and assuming it to be a hybrid produced by the union of a camel and a leopard, dubbed it " camelopard," which remains its heraldic name.

FIG. 80.—OSTRICH, TYGER, LION BICORPORATE AND COCKATRICE.

F

FIG. 81.—EGHAM.
*King John's crown and
Magna Carta.*

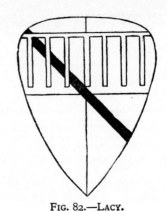

FIG. 82.—LACY.

VII

JOHN AND HENRY III

"A *Rose* may signifie unto us some kinde of *good* environed or beset on all sides with evils, as that is with prickels."

OF the central incident of King John's reign, his contest with the baronage on the question of feudal rights, we have heraldic record in the arms of Egham U.D.C., the district which includes Runnymede where the Great Charter was sealed. Egham's shield contains a representation of the Charter and King John's crown (Fig. 81) and the accompanying motto is, *Ut homines liberi sint*—"That men may be free."

Pro Magna Carta, the motto of the Despencers, tells that an ancestor helped to win the Charter; and one of the supporters of the Delaval shield is an armed man holding the Charter, representing an ancestor who was in arms against King John. These heraldic allusions to the Charter are, of course, modern. Thirteenth-century heraldry did not refer to current events, and even had it done so it was not likely that a baron would declare in his arms his opposition to the King.

The Twenty-five Barons.

Nevertheless, the arms of some of John's "five-and-twenty over-kings," chosen to supervise the execution of the Charter, are interesting because they show how one coat-of-arms sprang from another,

66

and reflect ties of kinship which drew some of the barons together into family groups.

Five of them bore chevrons derived from the arms of Clare (Fig. 16). The Clare chevrons themselves, red upon gold, were displayed by Richard, Earl of Gloucester, and Gilbert de Clare. Richard de Muntfichet, whose mother was a Clare, had three gold chevrons on red with a blue label. Robert FitzWalter, of Clare stock by paternal descent, varied the Clare arms by substituting a red fess for the middle chevron (Fig. 18), and similar arms appear on a seal of Saer de Quincy, Earl of Winchester, whose mother was widow of the Clare ancestors of the FitzWalters.

Quartered shields borne by four of the barons similarly indicate kinship. Robert de Vere, Earl of Oxford, had red and gold quarters with a silver star (Fig. 79), and his cousin, John de Lacy, Constable of Chester, bore the quarters gold and red with a black baston (narrow diagonal stripe) and silver label (Fig. 82). Geoffrey de Mandeville, Earl of Essex, whose lineage was intertwined with de Vere's, and Geoffrey de Say, whose mother was a Mandeville, both bore gold and red quarters.

The Cross of St. Patrick and FitzGerald.

After seven centuries the proud feudal arms just described survive only as quarterings in modern shields, or in the heraldry of a few cities and towns. But we have now to turn to an emblem which, while of small account among its thirteenth-century contemporaries, has become a part of the national flag.

The most notable memorial of the Anglo-Norman settlement in Ireland is the Irish national banner, the red saltire upon white which tradition associates with St. Patrick.

Unfortunately for tradition, St. Patrick had no more to do with the Cross of St. Patrick than the South Saxons had to do with the swallows of Sussex. The cross clearly originated in the arms of one of the greatest Irish feudal families, the FitzGeralds, who bore a red saltire on silver (Fig. 83).

In 1170, Maurice FitzGerald led an expedition to Ireland to help McMurrough, King of Leinster, against O'Connor of Connaught, who claimed to be King of Ireland. This FitzGerald's descendants became Earls of Kildare and Desmond, all leading spirits in Irish affairs, whether as Lords Deputy or " agin the Government."

The arms of the FitzGeralds were so intimately connected with great events in Irish history that they came to be regarded as national insignia, and associated with the national saint. And six and a half centuries after the FitzGerald saltire left England to seek its fortune in Ireland, it returned, canonised, to take its place in the Union Jack.

Another interesting reminder of the Anglo-Norman invasion is the shield of Munster, which contains three antique gold crowns on blue (Fig. 31). This, as told in Chapter III, was the banner of the East Anglian kingdom, whose martyr-king, St. Edmund, was greatly reverenced in the Middle Ages. This was the meaning attributed to the crowns by the fifteenth-century poet, Lydgate :

> " This other standard field stable of colour ind,
> In which of gold be notable crowns three,
> The first token in chronicle men may find
> Granted to him for royal dignity,
> And the second for virginity,
> For martyrdom the third in his suffering :
> To these annexed faith, hope and charity,
> In token he was martyr, maid and king."

In bearing St. Edmund's banner in their Irish expedition, the Anglo-Normans (like Richard II two hundred years later) perhaps had in mind that some of the Irish tribes had owned the authority of such pre-Conquest kings of England as could enforce it.

The three crowns came at a later date to be regarded as the arms of Ireland, and as such were introduced into the coinage by Edward IV (Fig. 173).

There are a few other reminders in Irish heraldry of the Anglo-Norman rule. Carlow, for instance, has for arms a castle over which flies a banner vertically gold and green and thereon a red lion rampant, the arms of the Bigods as Marshals of England (Fig. 84), who held

FIG. 83.—FITZGERALD.   FIG. 84.—THE MARSHAL OF ENGLAND.

territory there. The Bigods inherited these arms from their predecessors in the office of Marshal, the Earls of Pembroke.

The arms of Drogheda and some other Irish towns contain the
star and crescent which John adopted from Richard I's seal and placed
on the Irish coinage.

The Royal Supporters.

In Henry III's Great Seal we find the forerunners of the heraldic
supporters of the Royal Arms. Seated on his throne the King rests
each foot on a recumbent lion. This practice was continued in the
seals of his successors, but in the sixth seal of Edward III the lions
are seated on either side the throne.

From supporting the figure of the monarch, it was but a step to
making the lions support his shield. Henry VI is the first king known
to have used them in this way, and since his reign a lion has generally
been one of the " King's Beasts," while the other varied from time
to time until the Stuart period, when the Scottish unicorn became a
permanent royal supporter.

The Rose of England.

To Henry III's Queen, Eleanor of Provence, we owe the introduction of the rose into our national insignia. The rose of Provence
was of gold. A golden rose became the badge of Eleanor's eldest

FIG. 85.—RICHARD, EARL OF CORNWALL.
In Westminster Abbey.

FIG. 86.—DUCHY OF CORNWALL.

son, Edward I, while his brother, Edmund Crouchback, Earl of Lancaster, changed its colour to red for the sake of heraldic difference. The red rose of Lancaster, therefore, sprang from the same root as the royal golden rose.

Until the death of Richard II the golden rose remained a kingly emblem. When it withered with the failure of the line which bore it, its cousin, the red rose, contested for priority with a new-blown rose of white. The Wars of the Roses are the subject of a later chapter.

The Arms of Cornwall.

The arms of John's second son, Richard, Earl of Cornwall, Count of Poictou and King of the Romans (Fig. 85), consisted of a red lion rampant on silver within a black border containing a number of golden roundels. In later times these roundels, or bezants, were regarded as appertaining to the Earldom (now Duchy) of Cornwall, and it was therefore presumed that the Cornish arms consisted of fifteen bezants on black (Fig. 86). But Planché suggested that the bezants related not to Cornwall but to Richard's French county, being in reality golden peas (*pois*), in punning allusion to the name Poictou. If this be so, the arms of Cornwall are not of native but of foreign origin. They have, of course, by usage become the authentic arms of the Duchy, and they also appear in the shield of the Cornwall County Council, within a blue and white border denoting the county's sea-girt situation (Fig. 86a).

FIG. 86a.—CORNWALL COUNTY COUNCIL.

Cornwall's bezants, like the sheaves of the old Earldom of Chester, have been borne by Princes of Wales in their complete achievement of arms.   They also stand in the black border of the shield of Evesham, which thus acknowledges the good offices of Henry, Prince of Wales, son of James I, who secured the town's incorporation.   Within the border are the Prince's coronet and Chester wheatsheaf flanked by two of the famous ostrich feathers.

Lambeth, too, which embraces the extensive Kennington estates of the Duchy of Cornwall, has a black border with golden bezants, a tribute to Edward, Prince of Wales (now Duke of Windsor) and a link with his famous namesake, the Black Prince, who once occupied the old royal palace there (Fig. 49).

The Fight with the Favourites.

The arms of Pembroke College, Cambridge, recall the most unpopular of Henry III's imported Poictevins, William de Valence, Earl of Pembroke.   The College was founded by Mary de Chastillon, wife of William's son, Aymer, Earl of Pembroke.   The arms are an example of the process known as dimidiation, whereby half of the husband's shield is taken and joined to half of the wife's.   The De Valence arms were silver and blue bars with an "orle" (or inner border) of red martlets.   Those of Chastillon were red with pallets of vaire (fur represented by a white and blue design) and a gold chief with a blue label.   Fig. 87 shows how they are combined in the arms of the college.

Simon de Montfort, Earl of Leicester, the great leader of the nationalist movement against the foreigners, bore a white lion with a forked tail on red.   These arms are to be seen carved in stone in Westminster Abbey among shields of benefactors to the Abbey in Henry III's reign.   Since it is unlikely that the King would have De Montfort's arms set up after his revolt, it is assumed that the arms were carved before 1264—an instance of how heraldry sometimes helps us to assign a date to architectural work.

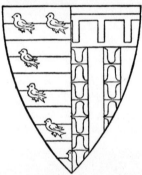

FIG. 87.—DE VALENCE and DE CHASTILLON *dimidiated:* the *arms of* PEMBROKE COLLEGE, CAMBRIDGE.

FIG. 88.—SIMON DE MONTFORT, EARL OF LEICESTER, *in West-minster Abbey.*

FIG. 89.—EDWARD I, *on his Great Seal.*

VIII

THE HAMMERING OF THE CELTS

" Edwardus Primus Malleus Scotorum Hic Est."
Epitaph of Edward I.

THE accession of Edward I, the first sovereign since the Conquest to bear an English name, marked " the emergence of the English." He made the throne the centre of the new national consciousness, and used this position to check the encroachments of the Church and the baronage on the Crown, and to establish England as the premier power in the island.

With regard to his internal activities heraldry is silent, but there are armorial reminders of his wars in Wales and Scotland.

Edward I in Wales.

The southern districts of Wales had long since passed into Anglo-Norman hands. Of the Marcher lords we still find traces in the place-name Montgomery, and in the chevrons of the Clare Lords of Glamorgan, which appear (between Tudor roses) in the arms of Glamorgan

73

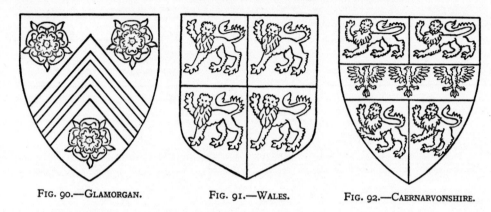

FIG. 90.—GLAMORGAN.   FIG. 91.—WALES.   FIG. 92.—CAERNARVONSHIRE.

County Council (Fig. 90), and the insignia of other places which were under the sway of the Clare family.

Radnorshire County Council surrounds the lions and boars' heads in its arms with a gold and blue border from those of Mortimer (Fig. 78), telling of the sphere of influence of that family, which later produced the Earls of March—the Welsh March.

Englishmen's heads in the arms of some old Welsh families are grisly reminders of the raids on English territory made by the Welsh princes in the intervals of their internecine warfare. Three such heads, cut off at the neck and set on red with an ermine chevron, tell that the family of Williams, later baronets of Penrhyn, sprang from Edynfed Fychan, who opposed the invasion of Ranulph, Earl of Chester. The heads of specifically *dead* Englishmen are borne by some of the Lloyds.

The survival of Welsh nationalism is reflected by the present-day arms of the principality of Wales, which are none other than those of the old princes of Gwynedd, including Llewellyn-ap-Griffith, who was slain at Builth, and his brother David, the last prince, who was executed at Shrewsbury. The shield is quartered gold and red, with four passant lions counter-coloured, *i.e.* red on the gold quarters and *vice versa* (Fig. 91). In the fifteenth century this was assumed by Owen Glendower, who claimed descent from Llewellyn and was the last champion of Welsh independence. It has been superimposed on the Royal Arms by Princes of Wales, marking the continuance of Wales as an historical and racial entity within the British realm.

Some patriotic Welshmen have asserted that the traditional motto of the Princes of Wales, *Ich Diene*, is not German, but a corruption of old Welsh words, *Eich Dyn*, meaning "Your man"—the words used by Edward I at Caernarvon when he presented to the Welsh people his infant son as a native Prince of Wales. Judgment must be left to those who have the Welsh tongue.

Edward I's three English lions still stand in the seal of Beaumaris, where he erected one of the strong castles built to keep the newly-formed counties in subjection.

The Caernarvonshire Eagles.

The arms of Caernarvonshire (Fig. 92) combine the four lions of the Principality of Wales with three golden eagles on a green fess. These eagles are from the arms attributed to Owen Gwynedd, King of North Wales. Since he died in 1169, it is unlikely that he actually used these arms, and although they have come to be regarded as his, it may be that we should turn elsewhere for their origin.

Now, on the first seal of Caernarvon, of late thirteenth century, an eagle appears above the lions of England. In 1371 an eagle was set up on the great tower of Caernarvon Castle, which came to be called the Eagle Tower. These facts suggest that the eagle was at this time an English royal emblem. It is perhaps significant that Henry III conferred "the honour of the Eagle"—old De Aquila's Pevensey—upon Prince Edward, who, as King Edward I, may have used this eagle as a badge. This would account for its appearance on the seal of Caernarvon and the castle tower, and so ultimately in the arms of the town. According to Michael Drayton, the men of Caernarvonshire marched under the banner of the eagles at Agincourt.

Edward I's grandson, Edward III, used an eagle as an extra crest, and passed it on to John of Gaunt, from whom, through the

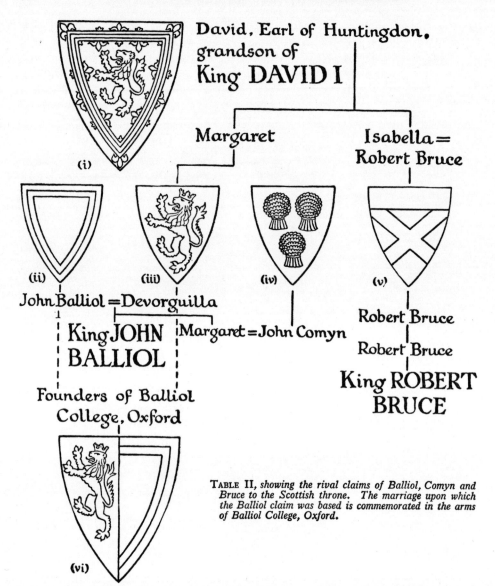

David, Earl of Huntingdon, grandson of **King DAVID I**

Margaret

Isabella = Robert Bruce

(i)

(ii)

(iii)

(iv)

(v)

John Balliol = Devorguilla

King JOHN BALLIOL

Margaret = John Comyn

Robert Bruce

Robert Bruce

King ROBERT BRUCE

Founders of Balliol College, Oxford

(vi)

TABLE II, *showing the rival claims of Balliol, Comyn and Bruce to the Scottish throne. The marriage upon which the Balliol claim was based is commemorated in the arms of Balliol College, Oxford.*

Beauforts, it descended to Christ's and St. John's Colleges, Cambridge. But the bird never became a notable royal symbol in England, which is as well in view of Erasmus's comment :

> " Of all birds the Eagle alone has seemed to wise men the type of royalty, a bird neither beautiful nor musical nor good for food, but murderous, greedy, hateful to all, the curse of all, and with its great powers of doing harm only surpassed by its desire to do it."

The Scottish Succession.

Soon after he had conquered Wales, Edward seized an opportunity of intervening in Scottish affairs. The death of Alexander III, followed by that of his granddaughter and heiress, Margaret, " the Maid of Norway," left the succession to the throne in dispute between thirteen claimants, of whom only two deserved and received serious consideration.

The families of Balliol and Bruce were both of Norman origin. Their genealogical position with regard to the Scottish royal house is shown by Table II, into which the appropriate coats-of-arms [1] have been inserted.

Edward I preferred Balliol, descended from the elder daughter of David, Earl of Huntingdon, before Robert Bruce (the first), who was a generation nearer the royal line. But he pressed his claims as suzerain too far, and drove Balliol into alliance with Philip the Fair of France.

[1] The arms are :

(i) The Royal Arms of Scotland (dealt with later).
(ii) A silver orle on red, for Balliol.
(iii) A white lion rampant with a golden crown on blue, for Devorguilla, heiress of Galloway.

These arms, (ii) and (iii), are to-day borne impaled by Balliol College, Oxford, (vi) founded by Devorguilla.

(iv) Three sheaves of barley (cummin) on red, for " Red " Comyn.
(v) A red chief and saltire on gold, the arms of Bruce. The number of Scottish families which still bear in their arms the chief and saltire, variously coloured and charged, is an indication of the high standing of the Bruces in the feudal hierarchy of Scotland. An instance is provided by the coat of Kirkpatrick (Fig. 98).

FIG. 93.—SCOTLAND.   FIG. 94.—FRANCE.

Scotland and France.

This alliance leads us to consider the Scottish Royal Arms (Fig. 93) which Balliol had assumed on becoming king. William Dunbar, in *The Thistle and the Rose* (1503), thus describes them :

> " This awfull beist full terrible of cheir,
> Persing of luke, and stout of countenance,
> Ryght strong of corpes, of fassoun fair, but feir,
> Lusty of shaip, lycht of deliverance,
> Reid of his cullor as the ruby glance.
> In field of gold he stude full myghtely
> With floure-de-lucis sirculit lustely."

The lion had for many years been the device of Scottish kings. It stood in the shield of Alexander III, and from the fact that his father, King William, was called " the Lion," we may assume that he too had displayed the beast. The tressure of fleurs-de-lys cannot, however, be traced with certainty to before the reign of Alexander III, and we may take it that the original arms of the Kings of Scotland consisted of a red lion on gold unadorned by flowers. This coat, in fact, is to-day borne by the MacDuffs, who claim to have sprung from the Celtic Kings of Scotland; and the families of Wemyss, Fife and Farquharson (Fig. 164) quarter it as evidence of descent from the MacDuffs.

How came the royal Scottish lion to stand within a floral tressure? This is generally supposed to signify an ancient alliance between Scotland and France, the fleur-de-lys being the French royal emblem. Fable has it that the alliance was made between Achaius of Scotland and Charlemagne, but this is unhistorical. Nevertheless, while the floral tressure cannot be traced to any specific alliance, it is clearly a heraldic symbol of that political understanding between England's northern and southern neighbours which was a recurrent factor in our history—an alliance which Shakespeare had in mind when he quoted from Holinshed,

> ". . . a saying very old and true :
> ' If that you will France win,
> Then with Scotland first begin.' "

The Scottish tressure in the arms of Cambridgeshire (of modern invention) recalls that successive Scottish monarchs held land in that part of England, and were in this way feudally dependent on the English king. The tressure and wavy bend (representing the River Cam) are gold on blue (Fig. 95).

FIG. 95.—CAMBRIDGESHIRE.   FIG. 96.—SETON, *commemorating the rescue of Bruce at Methven.*

FIG. 97.—WALLACE OF ELLERSLIE,
commemorating William Wallace.

FIG. 98.—KIRKPATRICK. *The shield
indicates feudal dependence on
Bruce, and the crest recalls the
murder of Red Comyn.*

William Wallace.

The traditional arms of William Wallace, who stirred up Scotland
against Edward I after Balliol's reduction, are a white lion on blue—
Scotland's beast in St. Andrew's colours. Wallace of Ellerslie to-day
bears a white lion on red within a white and blue border. The crest
is a mailed arm and hand grasping a sword, with the motto, *Pro
Libertate* (Fig. 97).

Robert Bruce.

After Wallace's defeat and death, Robert Bruce, grandson of the
first of that name to claim the Scottish throne, took up the sword.
The story of his quarrel with Red Comyn is recorded in heraldry by

the crest of Kirkpatrick. It is said that after Bruce had, in the Grey-friars Church at Dumfries, stabbed Comyn in a moment of passion, Bruce's follower, Kirkpatrick, committed the actual murder, saying, " I mak sikker (sure)," which words became the family motto of the Kirkpatricks, accompanying a crest of a hand grasping a dagger (Fig. 98). The pedigree (Table II) indicates the motive of the murder. Supposing the Balliols were passed over, Comyn would be a competitor for the throne which Bruce was determined to possess for himself.

Another incident in Bruce's career is supposed to be commemorated by the crest of the family of Johnstone, a winged spur. When Bruce was in England, before his seizure of the crown, Johnstone is said to have learned that Edward I intended him some mischief, and sent him a spur with a feather tied to it—a message which Bruce had no difficulty in interpreting : he fled at once. Such stories, of course, are more romantic than authentic. The Setons also claim armorial honours for an ancestor's service to Bruce. Sir Christopher Seton is said to have saved the King from capture at Methven, and to have won a red and blue shield with a sword supporting a crown within the Scottish tressure (Fig. 96).

The city of Aberdeen points to the silver tressure surrounding three silver castles in its red shield as a mark of Bruce's favour, while its motto, *Bon Accord*, is said to have been the watchword on the night when all the English in the city were massacred.

South of the border we find a relic of the Scottish wars in the shield of Appleby, its three crowned lions of gold on red, apparently based on the Royal Arms, having been assumed by the town, it is said, in allusion to its signal services against the Scots. (The field of the shield is sometimes recorded as blue.) Appleby's crest is a salamander, a creature reputed to be able to live in flames. This, with the motto, *Nec ferro nec igni*, befits a town which has shown that it can be destroyed " neither by sword nor by fire."

Edward I made two expeditions against Bruce. During the second he died at Burgh-upon-Sands. On his tomb in Westminster Abbey were inscribed the words which stand at the head of this chapter, together with his favourite motto, *Pactum Serva*—"Keep Troth."

G

The Hammering of the English.

Heraldry has little to say about Edward II. He bore, unworthily enough, the lions of his father, and as a badge a golden castle from the arms of his mother, Eleanor of Castile.

The armorial interest of his reign lies north of the Tweed, where Robert Bruce established himself as King of Scotland and hammered the English as he himself had been hammered. The arms of Stirlingshire (of modern invention) give us the heraldic record of the war's bloody climax at Bannockburn in 1314. They consist of a blue shield containing the white saltire of St. Andrew, and thereon the red

Fig. 99.—Stirlingshire, commemorating the Battle of Bannockburn.

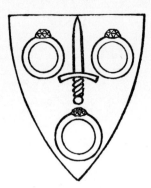

Fig. 100.—Seton.
The defence of Berwick.

lion of Scotland, the saltire being placed between two spur rowels and two caltraps (Fig. 99).

The caltraps were the means whereby the English chivalry (represented by the spur rowels) was overthrown at Bannockburn. A caltrap consisted of four metal spikes so arranged that however it lay on the ground one was always erect. The Scots scattered these weapons about the field to lame the English horses and throw their charge into disarray.

This stratagem was suggested by the Chief of the Clan Drummond, whose successors, the Earls of Perth, still place their shield on a ground strewn with caltraps, accompanied by the fitting motto, " Gang warily."

The motto of the Chief of the Clanranald, " My hope is constant in thee," is said to commemorate the remark passed by King Robert before the battle to the Lord of the Isles.

Bannockburn enabled Bruce to take the offensive against the English, and ushered in a long period of fierce and intermittent border warfare which has left its traces in the heraldry on both sides of the Tweed. The crest of the English family of Heselrigg, for instance, is a Scot's head ; and on the other side the Scottish Setons commemorate Sir William Seton's defence of Berwick against the English by adding a sword to their original arms of three gold rings on red (Fig. 100).

The Heart of Bruce.

Concerning the death of King Robert Bruce, the arms of the family of Douglas are a perpetual reminder of a romantic and beautiful story.

Froissart tells that when King Robert was " sore aged and feeble," he called to him Sir James Douglas, and told him that had he brought the realm to a state of peace he had purposed " to have gone forth and warred on Christ's enemies, adversaries to our holy Christian faith." Now, however, he was approaching death with his hopes unfulfilled.

> " And sith it is so that my body cannot go nor achieve that my heart desireth, I will send the heart instead of the body to accomplish mine avow. . . . I will that as soon as I am trespassed out of this world, ye take my heart out of my body and embalm it, . . . and present my heart to the Holy Sepulchre whereas our Lord lay, seeing my body cannot come there. . . . And wheresoever ye come, let it be known ye carry with you the heart of King Robert of Scotland at his instance and desire, to be presented to the Holy Sepulchre."

King Robert died on June 7th, 1329, and Douglas set forth by sea with the royal heart, " and kept always his post and behaviour with great triumph, with trumpets and clarions, as though he had been the King of Scots himself." To him, as he voyaged, came tidings that Alphonso, King of Spain, made war against the Saracen

King of Granada, and Douglas determined to break his journey to assist the Christians. When the battle was set,

> "he thought rather to be with the foremost than with the hindermost, and strake his horse with the spurs, and all his company also, and dashed into the battle of the King of Granada, crying, 'Douglas! Douglas!' weening to him the King of Spain and his host had followed, but they did not."

Douglas and his party found themselves surrounded. Froissart tells us they were all slain, and another chronicler states that Douglas cast the King's heart before him into the mêlée, and following it fulfilled Bruce's desire that he might lead a host against the infidel.

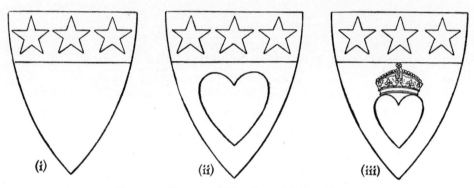

FIG. 101.—DOUGLAS: *The Care of Bruce's Heart.*

It is said that one knight escaped to bring the heart back to Scotland, where it was interred at Melrose Abbey.

In memory of this service to their King the Douglases added to their old silver shield with its three silver stars on a blue chief (Fig. 101 (i)) the red heart of Bruce (ii), which was later royally crowned (iii). These arms have been famous in Scottish history, and are referred to in many old ballads. Sir Walter Scott speaks of them :

> " The Bloody Heart blazed in the van,
> Announcing Douglas, dreadful name ! "

In later times the heart became familiar on our highways as the trade-mark of the Douglas motor-cycles.

Other families having a red heart in their arms have tried to associate it with this story. The Lockharts, for instance, claim an ancestor who carried a chest in which the King's heart lay, but their arms—a heart within a fetterlock—are clearly allusive to their name, and have no other significance.

Bruce's Armorial Epitaph.

The arms which are to-day borne by a branch of the family of Bruce recall the two kings of that great house and seem somewhat pathetically to dwell on the memory of past greatness. The supporters are a knight bearing in his hand a royal sceptre, and a lion with a crown upon his head and another about his neck. The crest is a mailed arm, the hand grasping a sceptre. The motto is *Fuimus*— "We have been."

On the death of David II the male line of the royal Bruces failed. By the marriage of his sister with the hereditary Lord High Steward of Scotland, the crown passed to the Stuarts. The Stuart (or Stewart) arms are a blue and white chequered fess on gold (Fig. 102). Various attempts have been made to explain these arms with reference to the feudal office which gave rise to the family name. An improbable explanation is that the chequers represent the napkin of blue and white design which the steward *may* have carried while performing his office ; an alternative and more likely suggestion is that they depict the chequered cloth which was spread upon the table of the " Exchequer " to facilitate computations.

In the old ballads the English and Scottish leaders are often denoted by their arms. These lines occur in a ballad of Otterburn, 1388 :

"The Bloody Heart in the Douglas arms,
    His standard stood on hie,
That every man might full well know ;
    Beside stood Starrès three.

The White Lion on the English part,
    Forsooth as I you sayn,
The Lucettes and the Crescents both,
    The Scots fought them again."

The lion and crescents were Percy emblems, and the " lucettes " were the pike-fish (luces) in the arms of Lucy, which the Percys bore following the Earl of Northumberland's marriage with the Lucy heiress.

Scotland and the Fleurs-de-Lys.

Before leaving Scotland for a time it will be convenient to deal with a curious attempt made by the Scottish Parliament in 1471 to remove the tressure from the Royal Arms. Parliament enacted that thenceforward the arms of Scotland should consist of the lion rampant only. But this Act was never put into operation.

The reason for its passage has puzzled heralds, but I think the political history of that very year contains the explanation. James III proposed to take a Scottish army to France to back King Louis against the Duke of Burgundy. The Estates of Scotland, however, would have none of the scheme, " pointing out to the King," says J. H. Burton, " that he had enough to do at home, and commenting on the questionable dealing of King Louis as to the countship of Xaintongue, which was to have been made over to the Crown of Scotland on his marriage with the daughter of James I."

The Scottish Parliament clearly did not favour intervention in French affairs, and the probable intention of the Act for the removal of the tressure from the arms was to abolish what was regarded as the outward and visible sign of the Franco-Scottish alliance. The survival of the tressure, despite the wish of Parliament, bears out this theory, indicating as it does the conflict of opinion between the King and his Estates.

The royal tressure is found in the arms of several notable Scottish families, being in some cases an indication of descent in the female line from the royal house, and in others a mark of honour conferred by the King for signal service.

Among those who bear it are the Bowes-Lyons, the family of Her Majesty the Queen Mother. The original shield of the Lyons contained a blue lion on silver; when Sir John Lyon, Secretary to Robert II and Great Chamberlain of Scotland, married the King's daughter, he was granted the royal tressure as an addition to his arms, which in this way became identical in design with those of the King, though different in colour. As events have shown, the arms were prophetic of a still more notable tie between his family and the royal house more than 500 years later. The crest of the Bowes-Lyons is a lady (King Robert's daughter) holding in her hand a thistle and surrounded by a bay-leaf garland.

Sir Walter Scott tells how Scott of Thirlestane won the tressure :

> " The treasured fleur-de-lys he claims
>   To wreathe his shield, since royal James,
>   Encamped by Fala's mossy wave,
>   The proud distinction grateful gave
>   For faith 'midst feudal jars ;
>   What time save Thirlestane alone,
>   Of Scotland's stubborn barons none
>   Would march to southern wars."

The motto of Thirlestane is " Ready, aye ready."

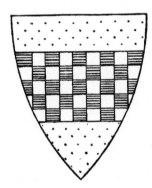

FIG. 102.—STUART.

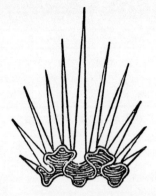

FIG. 103.—EDWARD III's SUNBURST.

IX

EDWARD III AND THE BLACK PRINCE

" Renownèd for their deeds as far from home,
For Christian service and true chivalry."

Shakespeare.

By contrast with the shame of Edward II's reign and the selfish misrule of his widow and her paramour, Mortimer, Earl of March, the accession to power of Edward III may be regarded as fittingly expressed by his favourite badge, a burst of sunshine through clouds (Fig. 103). But there was probably no conscious symbolism of this kind in the device. Mr. Fox-Davies has advanced the suggestion that it was merely a pun on Edward's birthplace, Windsor, the golden rays representing not the sun but *winds or* (gold). Against this theory we must set the fact that the badge was at an early date regarded and described as a " sunburst "; it is possible that Edward adopted Richard I's sun-badge as the basis of his own device, or it may be that without any thought of precedent he took the rays of the sun as the natural symbol of monarchy.

88

The Ostrich Feathers.

Another royal emblem of Edward III's reign, most notable because it is still a famous badge, was the ostrich feather.

A tradition which dates from not long after the battle of Crecy associates the origin of the Prince of Wales's feathers with the Black Prince, the oft-told legend being that they were borne, with the motto, *Ich Diene*, by the blind King John of Bohemia (who was slain) and assumed by the Prince as a memorial of his first great victory. But unfortunately for a popular and picturesque story—which, by the way, contemporary chroniclers ignore—ostrich feathers were not the crest of the Bohemian king, nor was *Ich Diene* his motto.

Equally baseless is Camden's statement that the Black Prince's feathers referred to " his speedy execution in all his services, as the posts in the Roman times were Pterophori, and wore feathers to signify their flying post-haste."

In fact the ostrich feathers did not originate with the Black Prince, nor was their use peculiar to him. They were also displayed by some of his brothers and their descendants, and we must turn for their first appearance in our royal heraldry to Edward III's marriage with Philippa of Hainault. It is believed that a coat-of-arms of black with three silver ostrich feathers was among this Queen's insignia, being probably allusive to Ostrevans, which was held by the Counts of Hainault.

Following the example of the three foregoing Edwards, who all adopted badges from their mothers' devices, the Black Prince took these arms as his " shield for peace " (Fig. 105), while his " shield for war " was, of course, the royal coat-of-arms differenced by a silver label (Fig. 104).

These two shields appear on the sides of his tomb in Canterbury Cathedral. The " shield for peace " is surmounted by a scroll with the motto *Ich Diene*, which also appears on the scrolls pierced by the pens of the feathers. If *Ich Diene* is German, as is generally supposed (despite Welsh claims), it means " I serve," and is thought to refer to the Prince's duty to the King, his father, " according to that of the

FIG. 104.—*The Shield for War.*   FIG. 105.—*The Shield for Peace.*

ARMS OF THE BLACK PRINCE,
from his tomb at Canterbury.

FIG. 106.—BADGE OF   FIG. 107.—SIR ROGER DE   FIG. 108.—BADGE OF
HENRY IV.   CLARENDON.   THOMAS OF WOODSTOCK.

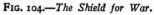

Apostle," wrote Camden : " ' The heir, while he is a child, differeth nothing from a servant.' "

The " shield for war " is accompanied by the old German word *Houmout*, meaning " Magnanimous," or, as rendered by " Toc H," who have made it their motto, " Hearts High."   It has been suggested that these two mottoes should be read in conjunction as " I serve with a high heart."

The effigy of the Black Prince on his tomb (Fig. 110) shows him with a surcoat of the Royal Arms.   Since the shield with the three feathers is definitely described as his " shield for peace," we may assume that on his peaceful occasions he wore a corresponding surcoat, the ground of which was, of course, black like the field of the shield. His nickname was therefore due to his black heraldic surcoat, and not to any habit of wearing black armour as is popularly supposed.

The Black Prince's illegitimate son, Sir Roger de Clarendon, who was hanged in Henry IV's reign for his fidelity to his half-brother Richard II, bore for arms the three feathers on a black bend in a gold shield (Fig. 107); and the crest of an eagle holding an ostrich feather was formerly used by a family which claimed descent from Clarendon, and distinguished their common patronymic by spelling it Smijth.

Many towns, especially Welsh towns, display the ostrich feathers in their arms in token of connection with divers kings or their heirs since Edward III.   Charged with a Tudor Rose, the feathers form the crest of Cardiff.   Carmarthen, Calne (Wiltshire) and Evesham are among other places which use them.

The Borough of Barnes, which contains White Lodge, where Edward, Prince of Wales (now Duke of Windsor), was born, commemorates him by bearing in its arms four white ostrich feathers. These are placed on a blue shield of which the central feature is a gold saltire charged with crossed oars, one dark and the other light blue, in allusion to the University Boat Race—a rare instance of an heraldic allusion to a sporting event.

During the Wars of the Roses, single feathers were used by individual Lancastrian and Yorkist members of the royal house, and these emblems took no particular side in the dynastic struggle between the red and white roses (Figs. 106 and 108 show variations of the single

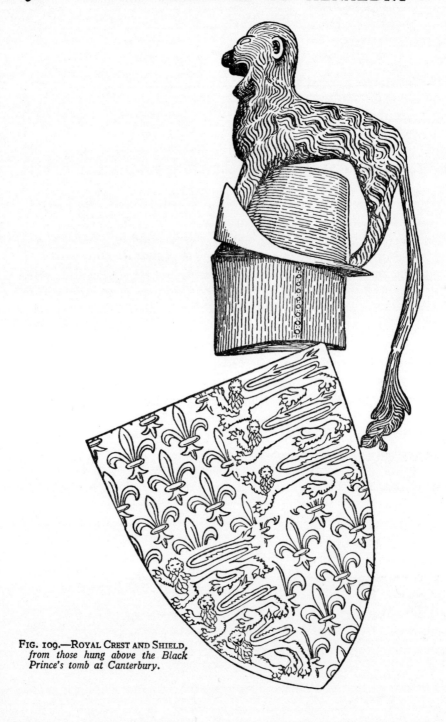

FIG. 109.—ROYAL CREST AND SHIELD,
*from those hung above the Black
Prince's tomb at Canterbury.*

feather). But the group of three feathers with the motto, *Ich Diene*, never became common property, and remains to this day the distinctive badge of the Heir Apparent.

Other badges of the Black Prince were the golden rose, and a swan with a lady's head, which was probably a device used in tournaments.

The Royal Crest of England.

The standing lion royally crowned, which is the Queen's crest, dates from the reign of Edward III, who, after an interval of a century and a half, revived Richard I's practice of bearing a lion on his helmet.

Richard's lion, as seen on his Great Seal (Fig. 71), was painted on the fan-shaped projection of his helmet. It was clearly derived from his grandfather, Geoffrey of Anjou, who had a lion on his cap (Fig. 57) and had received it from Henry I.

The four kings following Richard I do not seem to have used crests. They became the fashion in the fourteenth century with the elaboration of armour for the purposes of display, and Edward III followed the custom by having his lion modelled in boiled leather and placed on his helmet.

Edward's lion was not mounted upon a crown, as it is to-day, but on a cap; and it looked straight ahead as shown in Fig. 109.

Akin to the royal crest was the lion's face used as a badge by the Black Prince. It appears on the sword-belt on his effigy.

The Garter.

To Edward III we also owe the Garter with its motto, *Honi Soit qui Mal y Pense*, which surrounds the royal shield (Figs. 111 and 112).

Of the origin of the Most Noble Order we know little. According to its historian, Ashmole, it commemorated an occasion when King Edward had " given forth his own garter as the signal for a battle," which Ashmole takes to be Crécy. But this would place the date of the foundation too early.

A better-known theory associated the foundation of the Garter with a trivial mishap at a Court function, when the Countess of Warwick dropped a garter which the King, to cover her embarrassment,

FIG. 110.—THE BLACK PRINCE:
effigy on his tomb at Canterbury,
showing heraldic surcoat and crested
helmet, both " differenced " by the
label of the eldest son.

FIG. 111.—THE GARTER: *an early representation from a medallion showing the Black Prince before the Judgment Throne.*

FIG. 112.—THE GARTER, *from a brass.*

picked up and bound on his own leg, remarking, " Shame be to him who thinks ill of it."

This fable appears to have originated in France, and was perhaps invented to bring discredit on the Order. We are naturally unwilling to believe that the world's foremost order of chivalry had so frivolous a beginning, and we may more readily accept Froissart's account, though in placing the foundation of the Order as early as 1344 he is certainly at fault. He tells us :

" The King of England took pleasure to new re-edify the Castle of Windsor, the which was begun by King Arthur, and there first began the Table Round, whereby sprang the fame of so many noble knights throughout all the world. Then King Edward determined to make an Order and a Brotherhood . . . to be called Knights of the Blue Garter, and a feast to be kept yearly on St. George's Day."

So the Order may have been intended as a revival of the mythical

Round Table. Even so the symbolism of the garter itself remains obscure. A record of the Order compiled in Henry VIII's reign relates that Richard I, during his crusade, gave garters to certain knights as tokens of honour, and it was supposed that Edward III followed this example. But the legend has no good foundation. Ashmole regarded the garter as an emblem of " unity and society."

While Edward III may outwardly have professed the Order of the Garter to be a revival of the Round Table, it is probable that privately its formation was a move to gain support for his claim to the French throne. The motto of the Order is a denunciation of those who think ill of some specific project, and not a mere pious invocation of evil upon evil-thinkers in general. " Shame be to him who thinks ill *of it* " was probably directed against anyone who should oppose the King's design on the French crown. And it is significant that the colours of the garter—blue embroidered with gold—are those of the French Royal Arms. Furthermore, no French knights attended the feast of inauguration. All things considered, it seems highly likely that the Order originally represented the assembly of chivalry to aid King Edward of England to become King Edward of France.

Claim to the French Throne.

Edward gave heraldic expression to his claim to the throne of France when in 1340 he gathered the French fleurs-de-lys and set them in his own shield beside the English lions.

As early as 1331, soon after the French succession question first arose, Edward had incorporated the fleurs-de-lys in his second Great Seal, placing one on each side of his own enthroned figure ; but in the third seal, cut in 1338, the fleurs-de-lys were replaced by lions, Edward having for the time abandoned his French claims—at least, publicly.

Edward III pressed his claim against Philip VI on the slender pretext that, as nephew of Charles IV, he stood nearer to the throne than Philip, Charles's first cousin. He conveniently overlooked Charles of Navarre, his senior in the royal pedigree (Table III).

Seizure of the Fleurs-de-lys.

As the son of an heiress of the French Royal Family, Edward III was entitled to quarter the fleurs-de-lys with his three lions, placing

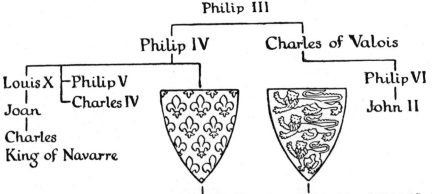

ISABELLA of FRANCE=EDWARD II of ENGLAND

EDWARD III

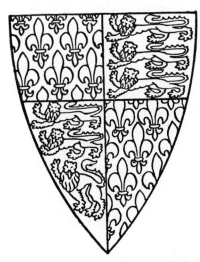

TABLE III, *showing Edward III's connection with the French Royal House on which he based his claim to the throne of France and incorporated the fleurs-de-lys in his arms.*

H

the French arms in the second and third quarters of his shield.   But in practice he gave the fleurs-de-lys precedence before the English lions, placing the latter in the second and third quarters, and the French arms in the first and fourth.   This was a clear expression in armorial terms of his claim to be King of France.

The Rev. E. E. Dorling, however, repeats a statement that Edward first placed the arms of France in the second quarter of his shield, but that King Philip protested : " It doth grieve us much, making apparent to the beholders that the little isle of England is to be preferred before the great realm of France."   But it is hardly likely that the French King would have urged his cousin of England to assume arms indicating a title to the French throne, or that Edward would have complied with a request so uncivilly worded.

Froissart tells us that Edward took the title and arms of France at the express wish of his Flemish allies ; that he was loth to do so without having conquered any part of France, but consented so that as titular King of France he could absolve the Flemings of their bond of two million florins in the Pope's chamber that they would not make war on the French king.

The " right " referred to in the English royal motto, *Dieu et mon Droit*, adopted by Edward III in 1340, was probably regarded by him as his right to the French throne.   It is, however, questionable whether he invented the famous motto, for it is said to have been used first by Richard I at the battle of Gisors, 1198, when he asserted himself to be no vassal of France but to owe his kingdom to God alone, and declared, " Not I, but God and our right have vanquished France." Perhaps Edward III had its anti-French meaning in mind when he made the motto his own.   And again, it is possible that Henry V quoted this motto in his speech to his army before Agincourt, in the passage rendered by Holinshed, " *God and our just quarrel* shall defend us."   But the motto did not come into permanent use until the reign of Henry VI.

Origin of the Fleurs-de-Lys.

The fleurs-de-lys of France continued to be quartered in our Royal Arms until the reign of George III, and are of frequent occurrence in heraldic compositions which are still in use.   Their history is therefore a matter of interest to us.

The fleur-de-lys in the form in which we know it is first encountered as the emblem of French royalty in the time of Louis VII (1120–80), and the most rational suggestions as to its origin are that it was derived from either the iris-flower or a spear-head. From the fact that it was early regarded as a flower most people accept the former theory. A thirteenth-century French writer regarded the central petal as representing Faith, guarded by the side petals of Wisdom and Chivalry. It has been suggested that the name fleur-de-lys, Anglicised as flower-de-luce, originally meant not lily-flower, but flower of Louis, its first wearer. Legend connects the emblem with an earlier Louis than the Seventh, namely, Clovis, King of the Franks, to whom the flower is said to have been brought by an angel in token of his accept-ance of Christianity. This story was put to practical use by the French Bishops at the Council of Trent (1545), when the question of precedence was in dispute. They alleged their King " to have been anointed King of the French and to have received the lily by divine authority."

Here the fleur-de-lys was clearly identified with the lily, and this is also the basis of the heraldic argument which (according to Guillim) was advanced to support the Salic law excluding from the French royal succession those who were descended through a woman. It was gravely argued that the crown of which the fleur-de-lys was the emblem could not pass through the female line because it was written of the lilies, " They toil not *neither do they spin*," " Which reason," wrote Guillim, " excludes as well a *Laborious Hercules* as a *Spinning Omphale*."

Dame Juliana Berners, in the *Boke of St. Albans*, tells us patriotically that the fleurs-de-lys were " geven to the foresayd Kyng of Fraunce in sygne of everlastynge trowble, and that he and his successours always with batayle and swordes should be punyshyd."

Another suggestion as to the origin of the fleurs-de-lys is that they were derived from three toads alleged to have been the arms of the Frankish kings. This idea perhaps gave rise to the nickname, " Crapaud Franchos," given to the French by their Flemish neigh-bours, and revived by our sailors in the last century in the form " Johnnie Crapaud," or plain " Froggy." The popular theory that this name arose from the alleged predilection of the French for the frog as a table delicacy is unfounded.

To-day we incline to a less distant and displeasing derivation of the famous flower, but in support of the theory that it developed from some Frankish ornament it may be recalled that when the tomb of Childerich, father of Clovis, was opened in 1653, some three hundred golden objects like bees, which had probably adorned the King's state robes, were found. This gave rise to the idea that bees were Frankish emblems, and Napoleon had this in mind when he substituted bees for fleurs-de-lys in the French arms, perhaps implying that he obliterated the Capetian and subsequent dynasties, and claimed to succeed to the Frankish kings.

About the year 1365, Charles V reduced the number of fleurs-de-lys in the French arms to three (Fig. 94), his professed reason being *pour symboliser la Sainte Trinite*, though it is possible that he also wished to make his arms different from those borne by the English kings in token of their claim to France, and thus take the sting out of the English arms. At the same time he was following the heraldic fashion of the period ; arms consisting of a field strewn with a single device many times repeated had been artistically effective for heraldic robes and surcoats, but shields and banners needed to be clearly distinguishable at a distance, and for this reason arms of this character were simplified.

If the French Kings thus hoped to rob the English Royal Arms of their significance they were disappointed, for in 1405 Henry IV reduced the number of fleurs-de-lys in *his* arms to three in each of the French quarters, thus reasserting his heraldic claim to the throne of France.

Until the accession of James I, our Royal Arms consisted of a quartered shield with three golden fleurs-de-lys on blue in the first and fourth quarterings, and three golden lions passant-guardant on red in the second and third. This shield is briefly described as France Modern and England quarterly.

The marshalling of the fleurs-de-lys of France beside the lions of England by Edward III was the signal for the outbreak of a war between the two countries which continued intermittently for a century. The armorial record of that war is next to be examined.

FIG. 113.—EDWARD III's NOBLE, *illustrating the development of Sea Power.*

FIG. 114.—DARTMOUTH.

X

THE FRENCH WARS

" Owre Kynge went forth to Normandy,
With grace and myght of chivalry;
The God for hym wrought marvelously,
Wherefore Englande may calle and cry,
Deo Gratias,
Deo gratias Anglie redde pro victoria."

DURING the Hundred Years' War formal chivalry reached its height and heraldry prospered greatly. Kings and great nobles began to mark their appreciation of special services by granting to some of their followers " honourable augmentations," consisting either of significant additions to existing arms or of new shields commemorative of special exploits; and the officers of arms maintained a careful supervision over all heraldic matters.

Growth of the Navy.

The French King determined to subdue Flanders and afterwards attack England, but this design was frustrated by the English naval victory at Sluys. This battle won for Edward III the title " Lord

101

of the Sea," which was confirmed to him by a victory over a Spanish fleet off Winchelsea in 1351. After this second battle, Edward had himself depicted in his character of sea-lord on his gold noble (Fig. 113) and silver coins.

The author of *A Libel of English Policie* wrote :

> " Four things our noble sheweth to me,
> King, Ship and Sword, and power of the Sea."

There is a striking similarity between the noble and the arms of Dartmouth (Fig. 114), a notable port which furnished many ships for

FIG. 115.—CINQUE PORTS.   FIG. 116.—HASTINGS.   FIG. 117.—IPSWICH.

Edward's wars. Dartmouth's red shield contains a golden ship's hull, with a seated lion at prow and stern, and Edward, in royal robes, between them.

For his naval forces, Edward, like his predecessors since the Conquest, relied mainly on the principal ports, especially those which were incorporated as the Cinque Ports. The position of the Cinque Ports as the mainstay of the King's navy, in return for special privileges, is reflected in their heraldry. The ancient arms of the corporation were three golden ships' hulls on blue; these were combined with the arms of England by the process known as dimidiation, that is to say, the " dexter " half of the English arms was joined to the " sinister " half of the shield of the ports, producing a shield

parted vertically red and blue and containing three golden lions
tailing off into three ships' sterns (Fig. 115).

Sandwich (one of the original Cinque Ports), Winchelsea and
Rye (which were incorporated later) bear these arms. Dover and
Deal embodied them in their seals, and the former still places a
border of English lions about its arms, which display St. Martin
and a beggar commemorative of St. Martin's Church, founded by
King Wihtred.

Hastings has varied the Cinque Port arms by eliminating the
middle hull, so as to leave one complete lion (Fig. 116). Ipswich
also uses a variation of them (Fig. 117), and Ramsgate and Margate

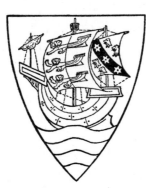

FIG. 118.—MARGATE.   FIG. 119.—TENTERDEN.   FIG. 120.—GREAT YARMOUTH.

(Fig. 118) have in their arms, with other charges, a single lion-hull.
The arms of Sandwich appear on the sail of a ship in the shield of
Tenterden (Fig. 119). Romney, one of the original ports, bears the
three lions of England on blue, having taken the blue field from the
old arms of the ports and abandoned the hulls in favour of complete
lions.

The arms of Yarmouth were formed, like those of the Cinque
Ports, by dimidiation of a shield with that of England, with the
curious result that the lions have herrings' tails (Fig. 120). Yarmouth
owes its very existence to the ancient herring fair, which was con-
trolled by the Cinque Ports, and it is fitting to find that the town's
original arms were three herrings on blue.

The town of Exmouth finds a place in its shield for the ten ships which it provided for Edward III's French expedition.

Caen, Crécy, Calais.

After Sluys there was a short truce, terminated by the dispute as to the succession to the Duchy of Brittany. In 1346 Edward again invaded France. The motto of the Radclyffe family, " Caen, Crécy, Calais," summarises the next stage of the war, and commemorates the part taken by Sir John Radclyffe in these famous victories.

The De la Bere family is one of several which use an ostrich feather plume as a crest and claim it to be a memorial of Crécy, where Sir Richard de la Bere is said to have rescued the Black Prince from danger. Confirmation is lacking. If every veteran of Crécy who subsequently wore a plume of feathers had rescued the Prince, he would have suffered more from the attentions of his friends than from the assaults of his enemies.

Poictiers.

The great battle of Poictiers has left heraldic record in the arms and devices of several families. The capture of the French King was attended by such confusion that doubt existed as to who had the honour of effecting it, claims being made by more than ten knights and esquires. But the part played by two Englishmen is witnessed by their heraldic emblems in the form of representations of parts of King John's weapons and equipment of war.

Sir John Pelham took as a badge the King's sword buckle, and this became the basis of a quartering in the Pelham shield in the seventeenth century—red with two silver pieces of belt with buckles attached (Fig. 121)—which is still quartered with three silver pelicans on blue (for Pelham) by the Duke of Newcastle and the Earls of Chichester and Yarborough. Sir John Pelham also used as a badge a caged bird in allusion to his royal captive.

The other Englishman concerned in King John's capture was Sir Roger de la Warre, who used as a memento of the event a badge

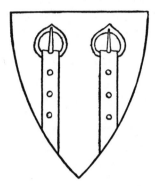

FIG. 121.—PELHAM.   FIG. 122.—DE LA WARRE.   FIG. 123.—MACKWORTH.

Memorials of Poictiers.

consisting of the crampet of the King's scabbard, bearing the letter " r " for *rex* (Fig. 122), and adopted as his motto the exultant cry, *Jour de ma Vie.*

The glorious part taken in this battle by the famous Lord Audley is chronicled by Froissart. Audley acknowledged the support he received from his esquires in the forefront of the battle by handing over to them the monetary reward he received from the Black Prince and by granting them heraldic honours. To one of them, Mackworth, ancestor of the baronets of that name, he gave a red chevron fretted with gold to bear on his black and ermine shield (Fig. 123), gold frets on red being the arms of Audley. Another squire, John de Delves, was given a similar chevron to place between the three black delves (or billets) on his silver shield.

Poictiers enabled Edward to secure temporarily the whole of the lands in the south of France which John and Henry III had lost. In return he relinquished all claim to the French throne, but the fact that he made no move to take the fleurs-de-lys out of his arms suggests that he intended to renew his pretensions when it suited him.

The Black Prince in Spain.

The subsequent campaign of the Black Prince in Spain has a reminder in our royal crown, which contains a large ruby said to have been given to Edward by King Pedro after the battle of Najara. Pedro had murdered the King of Granada for his jewels, and this stone was part of the spoil. The same ruby made an appearance at Agincourt, where Henry V wore it in the crown which turned the sword of the Duke of Alencon.

Agincourt.

Henry V's " sudden and hotte alarmes in France " are said to be symbolised by the flaming beacon which he bore as a badge.

" Agincourt " is the motto of the families of Lenthall, Walters

FIG. 124.—WODEHOUSE.

FIG. 125.—WALLER.

Memorials of Agincourt.

FIG. 126.—CODDRINGTON.

and Wodehouse, expressing their claims to have been represented at the chief battle of Henry's campaign.

John de Wodehouse's bravery at Agincourt is said to have won for him an armorial distinction which his descendants still display. He originally bore an ermine chevron and three ermine cinquefoils on black, but after this battle the chevron was gilded and scattered with drops of blood (Fig. 124).

Another interesting heraldic memorial of Agincourt is the crest of the family of Waller, of Groombridge, Kent. It was formerly a walnut tree, in rather strained allusion to the name. To this Richard Waller was privileged to add a shield of the arms of France differenced by a silver label—the shield of Charles, Duke of Orleans, whom Waller took prisoner at Agincourt (Fig. 125).

While singling out a few of his followers for special honours, Henry favoured all who were with him at Agincourt. In a severe writ dated 1418, directed against those who were using arms without ancestral right or authoritative grant, he excepts from the investigations of the sheriffs those *qui nobiscum apud bellum de Agincourt arma portabant*—" who bore arms with us at the battle of Agincourt."

" It is not unlikely," states Mr. Fox-Davies, " that Shakespeare had this writ in mind, or perhaps it was a matter of common knowledge in his day that use of arms at Agincourt was accepted as proof of gentility, when he put these words into King Henry's mouth on the eve of that great battle :

" We few, we happy few, we band of brothers ;
For he to-day that sheds his blood with me
Shall be my brother ; be he ne'er so vile,
This day shall gentle his condition."

John Coddrington, who was Henry V's standard-bearer " in battaile, watch and ward," bore a red fess and three red lions on silver ; in the following reign, for his good services and " to the worship of knighthood," his fesse was battlemented on both sides and fretted red on black (Fig. 126).

The Loss of France.

Having won recognition as the future ruler of France, and being officially styled by the French King, *Nostre treschier fil Henry roy d'Engleterre heretere de France,* Henry V emphasised the point in his heraldry, bearing the fleurs-de-lys in a shield by themselves, unaccompanied by his English lions. At his funeral his image was drawn in a chariot through the streets of London by four horses, the first caparisoned with the lions of England, the second with the quartered arms of England and France, the third with the French fleurs-de-lys, and the fourth with St. Edmund's three crowns, for Ireland. Of the last arms, Speed, who imagined them to have stood for King Arthur, said they were " well-beseeming him who had victoriously united three kingdoms in one."

FIG. 127.—SEAL OF HENRY VI, *with separate shield of French Arms indicating his claim to be king of France.*

Henry VI's seal shows that he continued his father's practice of displaying the arms of France separately from his own quartered shield, thus clearly asserting himself to be King of France; but the seal also indicates that he was characteristically unfitted to hold a conquered kingdom; for while the seals of all the other English kings of that warlike age showed them fully armed and vigorous upon horseback, brandishing their swords, that of Henry VI contained an angel supporting two shields—one of France and the other of France and England quarterly—as if to express his reliance on the heavenly hosts rather than on his own right arm to maintain him on the French throne (Fig. 127). His reputation for piety caused the next king of his name to sue the Pope for his canonisation, but the papal charge for a halo was regarded as excessive by the parsimonious Henry VII.

An heraldic passage in Shakespeare's *Henry VI* refers to the turning of the tide of victory against the English:

"Awake, awake, English nobility!
Let not sloth dim your honours new begot.
Crop'd are the flower-de-luces in your arms;
Of England's coat, one half is torn away."

Again, our failing fortunes at the siege of Orleans call forth this outburst from Talbot:

"Hark, countrymen! Either renew the fight
Or tear the lions out of England's coat;
Renounce your soil; give sheep in lions' stead;
Sheep run not half so tim'rous from the wolf . . .
As you fly from your oft-subdued slaves."

This is the period of the Maid of France. The arms conferred on Joan of Arc by Charles V were a blue shield containing a sword supporting a crown on its point, and on each side a golden fleur-de-lys (Fig. 128).

These arms recall Holinshed's statement that Joan wielded a sword " with five floure delices graven on both sides," which was mysteriously found among a heap of old iron in an ancient church. He says that her ensign was " all white, wherein was Iesus Christ painted with a floure delice in his hand."

Apt as her arms was the badge attributed to her, a crowned bee on a hive with the motto, *Hæc Virgo Regnum Mucrone Tuetur*— " This maiden defends the kingdom with a sword." After her death the badge of a phœnix, symbol of immortality and allusive to the manner of her martyrdom, was devised, with the legend, " Her death will make her live."

It does not appear that Joan ever used the arms granted to her, but they were borne by her brothers, upon whom Charles V conferred the honourable surname Du Lys.

FIG. 128.—Du Lys—*the family of* JOAN OF ARC.

FIG. 129.—HENRY IV'S STANDARD.

XI

THE BIRTH OF THE FACTIONS

" Might I but know thee by thy household badge."

Shakespeare.

The Hundred Years' War has carried us far beyond the reign of Edward III, and we must return to notice the beginnings of the faction strife which produced the shameful struggle known by the heraldic name, " The Wars of the Roses."

Seen from our special view-point, the rivalry which arose between the several lines of descent from Edward III appears to have been due purely to dynastic entanglements and the indefinite state of the law with regard to the succession to the throne. But to preserve historical perspective it is well to remark that the legal issues between York and Lancaster were the occasion rather than the cause of hostilities. The true cause lay in the personal ambitions of a few Goliaths among the greater baronage, who, by inbreeding, had amassed lands and dignities until their state rivalled that of the Crown itself.

The Nevilles, the Percys and the Mortimers represented the rank growth of feudalism which was sapping the sovereign power. By marrying his numerous sons to heiresses of great nobles Edward

110

tried to re-establish the royal supremacy, but only succeeded in introducing elements of discord into the royal house itself, and these rent his descendants into two camps. Outworn feudalism fell by sword and axe, dragging with it the feudal monarchy of the Plantagenets.

Livery and Maintenance.

The most notable heraldic feature of the period into which we are now to enter is the widespread use of badges. While the arms and crest were personal to the individual and ought not to be used by anyone else (except that cadets used the arms of the head of the family with proper difference), the badge might be worn by a noble-man's retainers, and during this century of baronial anarchy the badge a man wore was significant of his political sympathies.

This great increase in the use of badges was the outward sign of the pernicious customs known as livery and maintenance. " Livery was originally the allowance (*liberatio*) in provisions and clothing which was made for the servants and officers of the great households, whether of baron, prelate, monastery or college " (Stubbs). In due course the term livery came to be applied only to the gift of clothing, and then to the colours or " household badge " that the man adopted to mark his adherence to a particular lord. The nobles freely granted leave to wear their livery or badge to all who asked it, thus gathering about them a large number of men on whom they could call at need, and granting in return their protection and maintenance, especially in case of litigation. The extensive use of badges, therefore, was a sign of the growth of factions within the State, and of unconstitutional means to defeat the ends of justice.

A political poem of 1449 shows how closely the great nobles were associated in men's minds with the badges they used. We read, for instance, of Lord Willoughby, " Our myllesaylle will not abowte "; of Holland, Duke of Exeter, " the firy cresset hath lost its lyghte "; of Neville, Earl of Kent, " the Fissher hath lost his Hangulhook "; and of Talbot, Earl of Shrewsbury, " he is bownden that our dor shuld kepe, that is Talbott, our good dogge." The

FIG. 130.—STAFFORD.　　　　FIG. 131.—WESTMINSTER.

unpopular William de la Pole, Duke of Suffolk, who was beheaded
at sea in 1450, is referred to by his badge, " the Ape clogge," whence
the contemptuous nickname given him, " Jack Napes "—the origin
of our " jackanapes."

Some feudal badges survive to-day in the arms of municipalities.
The town of Stafford, for instance, displays in its shield the knot
which was the badge of the Stafford family, and it is unjustly alleged
by the men of neighbouring places that this knot, comprising three
loops, signifies that the Stafford men were such rogues that arrange-
ments had to be made to hang them three at a time (Fig. 130).

Royal Badges.

Edward III was the first king to make use of many badges.　In
addition to those mentioned in Chapter IX he had a gold tree-stump
(allusive to the royal manor of Woodstock), a falcon, a gryphon and
a boar.

The several branches of the Royal Family descendant from him
can best be dealt with in tables with heraldic notes, to which reference can be made in connection with the dynastic matters raised in
the following chapters, where the historical associations of the various
badges are more fully discussed.

TABLE IV.—THE WHITE HIND AND THE WHITE HART.

EDWARD III

Sir Thomas Holland = Joan 'the Fair = Edward 'the
Earl of Kent | Maid of Kent | Black Prince'
Badge: A
White Hind

Thomas Holland   John Holland   RICHARD II
Earl of Kent . Badge: Badges: A White
A White Hind   Hart . Sun, etc.

Richard II used as badges, among others, a white hart derived from his mother's white hind ; a sun-in-splendour, perhaps a development of his grandfather's sun-burst, or perhaps taken from the second seal of the first Richard ; and *planta genista* with empty cods, indicating his childless state.

The white hart and suns appear on his standard (Fig. 137), which is typical of the ceremonial standards of the time, containing the cross of St. George on white next the staff, and badges on the long tapering part. Richard's standard was divided lengthwise into white and green, and bore the royal motto in gold. The border was also white and green.

In the play, *Richard II*, Shakespeare makes several references to the royal sun-in-splendour. For instance, Salisbury says to the King :

" Thy sun sets weeping in the lowly west,
    Witnessing storms to come, woe and unrest."

I

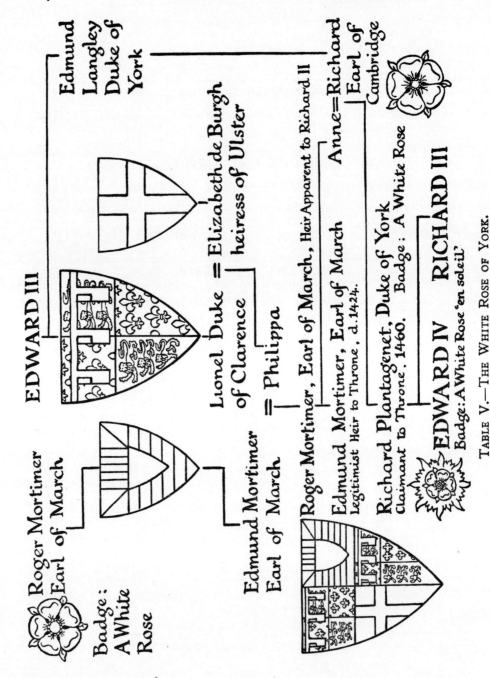

TABLE V.—THE WHITE ROSE OF YORK.

TABLE VI.—THE RED ROSE. (i) *The Lancastrian Kings.*

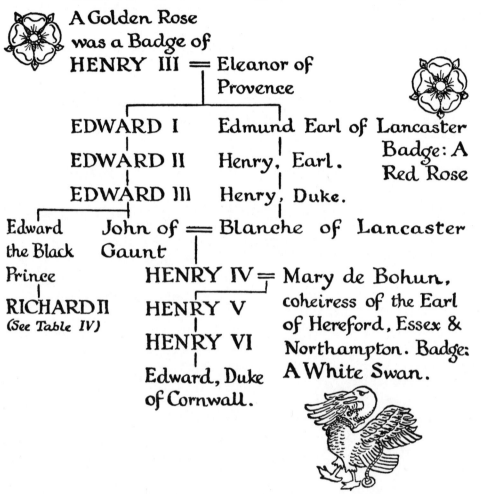

A Golden Rose was a Badge of HENRY III = Eleanor of Provence

EDWARD I   Edmund Earl of Lancaster

EDWARD II   Henry, Earl.   Badge: A Red Rose

EDWARD III   Henry, Duke.

Edward the Black Prince   John of Gaunt = Blanche of Lancaster

RICHARD II (See Table IV)   HENRY IV = Mary de Bohun, coheiress of the Earl of Hereford, Essex & Northampton. Badge: A White Swan.

HENRY V

HENRY VI

Edward, Duke of Cornwall.

The badges of the Lancastrian Kings included the ostrich feather (which Henry IV entwined with a scroll bearing the word SOVEREYGNE —Fig. 106), the eagle used by Edward III as a private crest, the *planta genista* with genet cat (Chapter V); the red rose of Lancaster, sometimes placed within a sun; the white swan of the Bohuns, who had it from the Mandevilles; and also an antelope, the letters SS, a columbine flower, crowned panther, cresset light, and fox's brush.

Shakespeare possibly had the eagle badge in mind when in *Henry VI* he made the Duke of Gloucester address the young Prince Edward thus :

> " Now if thou be that princely eagle's bird,
> Show thy descent by gazing at the sun."

The red rose, swan, tree-stumps and foxes' brushes appear on Henry IV's standard, set on white and blue, the Lancastrian livery colours (Fig. 129).

The fox's brush, according to Camden, related to " Lysander's advice, if the Lyon's skin were too short to piece it out with a Foxes case."

Partisans of the House of Lancaster sometimes wore livery collars composed of the letters SS (Fig. 138), frequently with a pendant white swan. This famous collar, which survives to-day as part of the insignia of the Lord Chief Justice, Sergeants-at-Arms, Kings-of-Arms, and the Lord Mayor of London, has been the subject of much discussion. To give one instance of the various theories about it, Camden believed the SS to stand for *Sanctus Simo Simplicius*, a Roman lawyer, and says the collar was the special emblem of members of the legal profession. But plain fact seems to be that the collar was nothing more than a development of Henry IV's badge of SS. Some of the collars (like Henry IV's ostrich feather) bore the word SOUVERAIN, and some the words SOVEIGNEZ VOUS DE MOY, so the SS signified either loyalty or remembrance.

In support of the view that they stand for SOUVERAIN, a curious anecdote of Henry V's youth is worth quoting. Learning that his father was grieved at his loose practices and doubted his loyalty, Prince Henry went to court (Speed tells us) dressed in " a Gowne of blew satten wrought full of *Eylet-holes*, and at every *Eylet* the Needle left hanging by the silke it was wrought with ; and about his arme he ware a *dog's-collar* set full of SS of Gold, the *Girets* thereof being most fine Gold." The collar of the King's badge of SS was probably intended to express his continued loyalty, and should be taken together with these words from the submissive speech which the Prince addressed to the King : " The name of *Soveraigne* ties allegiance to all." The eyelets may have expressed his vigilance against those who slandered him, while the needles were perhaps a threat to punish them.

As supporters of the Royal Arms Henry VI used variously white antelopes, a lion and panther, and a lion and antelope.

TABLE VII.—THE RED ROSE. (ii) *The Beauforts.*

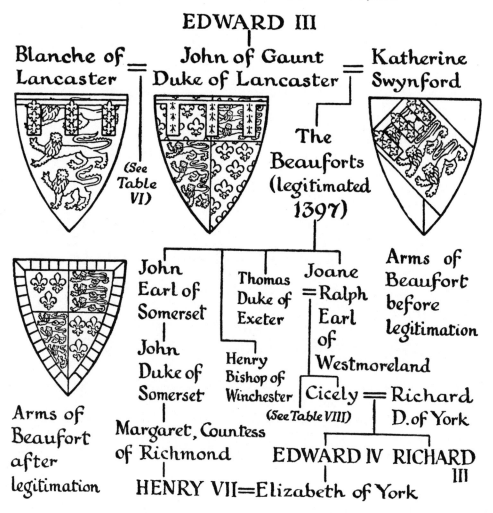

EDWARD III

Blanche of = John of Gaunt = Katherine
Lancaster   Duke of Lancaster   Swynford

(See Table VI)

The Beauforts (legitimated 1397)

John Earl of Somerset

John Duke of Somerset

Thomas Duke of Exeter

Henry Bishop of Winchester

Joane = Ralph Earl of Westmoreland

Arms of Beaufort before legitimation

Arms of Beaufort after legitimation

Margaret, Countess of Richmond

Cicely = Richard D. of York
(See Table VIII)

EDWARD IV   RICHARD III

HENRY VII = Elizabeth of York

The Beaufort badges were a white ostrich feather, the quill blue and white (the Lancastrian colours), and a portcullis. The latter emblem has survived to form the crest of the present Duke of Beaufort, surnamed Somerset, who is descended from Charles Somerset, a natural son of Edmund Beaufort, Duke of Somerset. The portcullis became chiefly famous through its extensive use by Henry VII (Chapter XV), from whom it passed into the arms of the City of Westminster (Fig. 131), and became the badge of the Palace of Westminster. Having thus come to be associated with the seat of Parliamentary government, it has been adopted as the crest of Canberra, the Australian capital.

As legitimist heirs of Richard II, through Anne Mortimer, the Dukes of York and Yorkist Kings used as badges the sun-in-splendour and the white hart, the white lion of the earldom of March, the black dragon of the earldom of Ulster, and the black bull of the Honour of Clarence. Their white rose was also probably a Mortimer emblem. From Edmund Langley they received the falcon and the fetterlock. Richard III used as a badge a white boar.

Livery collars worn by Yorkist partisans, as a counterblast to the Lancastrian collar of SS, were generally composed of alternate suns and white roses (Fig. 139). Various pendants were used, the lion of March and the white boar of Richard III being the most common.

As supporters of the Royal Arms, Edward IV used a white or gold lion and a black bull; and Richard III used a gold lion and white boar, or two white boars.

Edward III's sixth son, Thomas of Woodstock, Duke of Gloucester, married Eleanor Bohun, the sister of Henry IV's queen. Their only daughter Anne married firstly Edward, Earl of Stafford, and secondly William Bourchier, Earl of Eue, and carried to both families the famous white swan badge. Fourth in descent from this Earl of Stafford was Edward, Duke of Buckingham, "the beautiful swan" whose death was compassed by Cardinal Wolsey (Chapter XV). The white swan on a field black and red still forms the arms of the town of Buckingham (Fig. 167), and also appears in the shields of Buckinghamshire County Council and High Wycombe, Bucks.

FIG. 132.—ARMS OF RICHARD II,
embodying those of Edward the Confessor.

XII

RICHARD II

" See, see, King Richard doth himself appear,
As doth the blushing, discontented sun
From out the fiery portal of the east."

Shakespeare.

DURING the reign of Richard II the Royal Arms underwent a temporary change, being marshalled on a shield beside those of Edward the Confessor (Fig. 132). Froissart attributed this practice to political reasons connected with Ireland, but this explanation does not account for the display of the Confessor's arms in England. When Richard rebuilt Westminster Hall he had St. Edward's shield, together with his own badges, carved in the roof, where they stand to-day; and he also granted them as an heraldic honour to several noblemen. Clearly Richard II, for some reason we cannot fathom, held the Confessor in special regard, and took his arms with some deeper feeling than the desire to create an impression in Ireland, though this may have been part of his motive.

Froissart's story, on the authority of a squire named Christead, is as follows :—" Saint Edward, King of England, lord of Ireland

119

and of Acquitaine, the Irish loved and dued him much more than any other King of England that had been before; and therefore our sovereign lord King Richard this year past, when he was in Ireland, in all his armories and devices he left bearing the arms of England, as the libbards and flower-de-luces quarterly, and bare the arms of this Saint Edward, that is a cross potent gold and gules with four white martinets in the field;[1] whereof it was said the Irishmen were well pleased, and the sooner they inclined to him; for of truth the predecessors of these four kings (of Ireland) obeyed with faith and homage to the said King Edward, and they repute King Richard a good man and of good conscience, and so they have done to him faith and homage as they ought to do, and in like manner as their predecessors sometime did to Saint Edward."

It is true that pre-Conquest kings had occasionally received from small portions of Ireland some acknowledgment of their overlordship, and this heraldic instance shows that later monarchs had elaborated this fact into a large argument to support their conquest of the eastern part of the island. We need not discredit the story merely because these arms had not existed in the Confessor's own lifetime; the fact remains that they had become definitely associated with him, and Richard's assumption of them would therefore be effective as an indication of his claim to that obedience which was traditionally rendered to St. Edward.

A representation of Richard II's banner, embodying the Confessor's arms, appears on the brass of his standard-bearer, Sir Simon de Felbrigge, in Felbrigg Church, Norfolk (Fig. 133).

Grants of Edward the Confessor's arms as marks of honour were made to the King's two half-brothers (the Hollands, Earl of Kent and Duke of Exeter) and to Thomas Mowbray, Duke of Norfolk.

Robert de Vere, Earl of Oxford, whom Richard created Lord of Ireland and Marquis of Dublin, was granted as an augmentation the three crowns of Ireland within a silver border, to be quartered with his own paternal coat (Fig. 134).

[1] Froissart is at fault in his description of the arms—see Chapter III. Moreover, Richard did not cease to use his lions and fleurs-de-lys, but bore the Confessor's arms in addition.

FIG. 134.—DE VERE,
*with augmentation as Lord of
Ireland.*

FIG. 133.—SIR SIMON DE FELBRIGGE,
with Richard II's banner.

A permanent heraldic memorial of Richard's Irish expedition
(during which the kingdom of England was seduced from its allegiance by his cousin, Henry Bolingbroke) is the present crest of Ireland—
a white hart springing from a triple-turreted tower (Fig. 135). The
white hart was Richard's favourite badge, derived from his mother's
white hind (Table IV). From this famous badge many inns
derive their name and sign. It is probable, too, that here we have
the origin of the arms of Derby, a hart sitting in a ring fence on a
green shield.

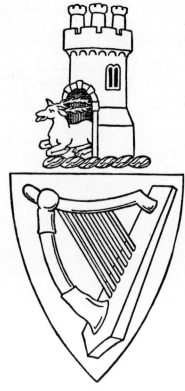

FIG. 135.—IRELAND.

FIG. 136.—THE FALCON AND
FETTERLOCK.

FIG. 137.—RICHARD II's STANDARD.

The Succession Question.

Richard II's nearest kinsman and heir-apparent was Roger Mortimer, Earl of March, on whose death Edmund, Earl of March and Ulster, became the heir (Table V.). Descended from Lionel of Clarence, Edward III's third son, Edmund was entitled to quarter in his shield the Royal Arms with the Clarence label, together with those of Mortimer and Ulster. In practice he was content to bear only the two latter coats (Fig. 140), perhaps fearing to provoke the hostility of the junior branches of the Plantagenet House by too openly vaunting his position as heir to the throne by displaying the Clarence shield. However, whether used or not, that shield was his rightful inheritance, and throughout the fifteenth century its possession, together with the arms of Mortimer and Ulster, denoted a legitimist title to the throne.

Edmund had good reason to fear the enmity of his Plantagenet cousins, the descendants of Edward III's younger sons, for though Edward III himself had claimed the French throne by preferring female descent in the senior line before male descent in the junior, this principle was open to contest, and true Plantagenets like the sons of John of Gaunt and Edmund Langley would not consent to be ruled by a Mortimer, who was Plantagenet only on the spindle side.

After King Richard II, the senior descendant in the male line from Edward III was Henry Bolingbroke. He bore the Royal Arms with a label partly ermine, like that of his father, John of Gaunt, and partly blue with fleurs-de-lys, like his mother's (see Tables VI and VII). His presence in England was a menace to Edmund Mortimer's succession, and Richard found an excuse for exiling him.

The Falcon Imprisoned.

Henry Bolingbroke's half-brothers, the Beauforts, were of illegitimate origin, and though legitimated were held to be incapable of succeeding to the throne; so that beside the King, old Edmund Langley, Duke of York, and his sons found themselves the sole descendants of Edward III in the legitimate male line resident in

England. Little wonder was it that the two young men, Edward of York and Richard of Cambridge, speculated on their chances of occupying the throne, and they were not discouraged by their father, if we are to believe a heraldic anecdote. Edmund Langley bore as a badge a falcon, inherited from Edward III, which he displayed within a fetterlock (Fig. 136—from Westminster Abbey). This imprisonment of the bird is supposed to have meant that Langley " was locked up from all hope and possibility of the kingdom when his brethren began to aspire thereto. Whereupon he asked on a time his sons, when he saw them beholding this device set up in a window, what was Latin for a fetterlock; whereat, when the young gentlemen studied, the father said, ' Well, if you cannot tell me, I will tell you : *Hic, hæc, hoc, taceatis ;* ' as advising them to be silent and quiet; and therewithal said, ' yet God knoweth what may come to pass hereafter.' "

Legitimist Risings.

The succession question was rudely settled for the time by Boling-broke's return to seize the throne, Richard II's enforced abdication, and his tragic death.

The white hart lingered on after Richard's fall, being borne openly or in secret by some who remained faithful to him. According to Holinshed, " among the few friends who attended this unfortunate prince after his capture by the Earl of Northumberland was Jenico d'Artois, a Gascoigne, that still wore the cognisance or device of his master, King Richard; that is to say, a white hart; and would put it away from him neither by persuasion nor threats; by reason whereof, when the Duke of Lancaster understood it, he caused him to be committed to prison within the castle of Chester. This man was the last (as saith mine author) which wore that device, which showed well thereby his constant heart towards his master."

Nevertheless, on rumours of Richard's survival in Scotland the Countess of Oxford and others of his adherents secretly wore the white hart in token of their enduring allegiance.

To the revenge of the white hart came the white hind—Holland,

Earl of Kent—but was captured and beheaded. Then rose Owen Glendower, his head full of symbolic prophecies of Merlin :

> " . . . of a dragon and a finless fish,
>   A clip-winged griffin and a moulting raven,
>   A couching lion and a ramping cat."

Shakespeare based these lines on a heraldic passage in Holinshed, who wrote that Glendower, Percy and Mortimer caused a tripartite indenture to be made, thus giving credit to " a vaine prophesie, as though King Henrie was the mouldwarpe, curssed of God's owne mouth, and they three were the dragon, the lion and the woolfe which should divide this realme between them."

The meaning of the passage is clear when we remember that Glendower's badge was the Welsh dragon, while Percy bore the blue lion of Louvaine, and a wolf was a badge of the Mortimers.

The rebels were defeated at Shrewsbury, where Henry IV, knowing himself to be marked out for his enemies' special attention, gave Sir Walter Blount and some others the perilous honour of wearing surcoats of the Royal Arms.

" I marvell to see so many kings thus suddenlie arise one in the necke of another," exclaimed the Earl of Douglas, who, according to Holinshed, slew four of them with his own hand.

The later rising of Richard, Earl of Cambridge, in the legitimist cause was due to his marriage with Mortimer's sister Anne, which placed him within the line of succession should Mortimer die without heir. He went to the block; but left a son, Richard Plantagenet, later Duke of York, who, in the reign of Henry VI, came forward openly as the legitimist claimant, and set up the white rose in opposition to the red rose of Lancaster (Table V).

FIG. 138.—THE LANCASTRIAN COLLAR OF SS.

FIG. 139.—THE YORKIST COLLAR OF SUNS AND ROSES.

XIII

THE RIVAL ROSES

" . . . I prophesy : this brawl to-day . . .
Shall send between the red rose and the white,
A thousand souls to death and deadly night."

Shakespeare, *Henry VI.*

THERE is a popular but erroneous idea that the red and white roses of the rival Houses of Lancaster and York originated in the scene in the Temple Gardens between John Beaufort, Duke of Somerset, and Richard Plantagenet, which was narrated by Shakespeare in *Henry VI* and portrayed in the famous picture in the Houses of Parliament.

According to Shakespeare, Somerset and Plantagenet were quarrelling on the succession question, and appealed thus to their companions :

126

"*Plantagenet.*   Let him that is a true-born gentleman,
And stands upon the honour of his birth,
If he suppose that I have pleaded truth,
From off this briar pluck a white rose with me.

Somerset.   Let him that is no coward and no flatterer,
But dare maintain the party of the truth,
Pluck a red rose from off this thorn with me."

Whereupon their followers plucked the flowers on the understanding that the disputant who received the lesser support should yield. Three white roses were gathered, and only one red one. Plantagenet therefore asked :

"Now, Somerset, where is your argument?

Somerset.   Here, in my scabbard, meditating that
Shall dye your white rose to a bloody red."

There is no suggestion in Shakespeare's account that this incident (if it ever occurred) gave rise to the rival emblems ; and in fact the red and white roses were in use as badges long before the famous quarrel. So we must read Shakespeare as meaning that Somerset plucked the red rose and Plantagenet the white because these roses were already the badges of their respective houses.

We have seen that a golden rose had been a royal badge since its introduction into our heraldry by Eleanor of Provence, Henry III's queen. It was a badge of the three Edwards, it appears on the canopy of the Black Prince s tomb, and Richard II inherited from his father a blue vestment embroidered with ostrich feathers and golden roses. Froissart tells us that a book of " amours and moralities " that he had engrossed for presentation to Richard II was " covered with crimson velvet, with ten buttons of silver and gilt, and roses of gold in the midst." Shakespeare may have had this royal emblem in mind when he referred to Richard as " that sweet, lovely rose." So the golden rose is clearly traceable down to Richard II, at whose death it faded.

The red rose was a cousin of the rose of gold. It had clung to the title of Lancaster since its adoption by Edmund Crouchback, second son of Eleanor of Provence. When the Lancastrian heiress, Blanche, married John of Gaunt, she carried the red rose to him, and it became the distinctive badge of his descendants, the Lancastrian kings and the Beauforts (Table VI).

Various suggestions have been made to account for the use of a white rose by the House of York. Planché thinks it was originally a Clifford badge; but it is a fact of greater significance that a white rose was the badge of Roger Mortimer, grandfather of that Roger who was Richard II's heir. It was by his Mortimer descent that Richard Plantagenet could claim the throne, and it therefore seems most probable that he took his white rose from the Mortimer emblem, selecting that particular emblem from among his various badges because it seemed the most appropriate to oppose to the red rose of Lancaster (Table V).

Shakespeare makes Richard Plantagenet soliloquise :

> " Then will I raise aloft the milk-white rose,
>   With whose sweet smell the air shall be perfumed ;
>   And in my standard bear the arms of York,
>   To grapple with the house of Lancaster."

Before the white rose came into prominence, Richard was known by his falcon badge, and a satire of the time says of him :

> " The Fawkon fleyth and hath no rest
>   Tille he witte wher to bigge his nest."

As Planché remarked, the colours of the rival roses were the more significant because they corresponded with the livery colours of the Plantagenets—white and red—and thus reflected the split in the family.

In the light of history we may assign significance to the two roses which those who bore them did not associate with them. The red rose appears to us as the symbol of Parliamentary sanction by which the Lancastrians held their crown, while we may regard the white rose as the emblem of strict legitimism. In the same way the arms of the Beauforts and the House of York illustrate these rival principles.

Beaufort Heraldry.

The original arms of the Beauforts clearly indicated their illegitimate origin. They consisted of a shield divided vertically white and blue—the Lancastrian colours—with a broad red bend charged with the arms of the Duchy of Lancaster: the lions of England with a blue label strewn with the fleurs-de-lys. It seems hardly fitting that John of Gaunt gave his illegitimate sons a shield based on the colours and arms of his first wife (Table VII).

In 1390, following the marriage of their parents, the Beauforts were legitimated by Act of Parliament, and changed this shield for the Royal Arms differenced by a blue and white border. This border was not a definite sign of illegitimacy; nevertheless the usual way of differencing the Royal Arms was by a label or plain border (sometimes charged with fleurs-de-lys), and it seems that the assignment of a parti-coloured border to the Beauforts was intended to place their arms on a lower level than those of families of unimpeachable royal descent.

The Act of Legitimation was confirmed by Henry IV *excepta dignitate regali,* but this clause, clearly barring the Beauforts from the throne, was omitted from the document laid before Parliament, and therefore could be held to be ineffective by those who stood for Parliamentary sanction in questions of succession to the throne.

The Arms of York.

While the heraldry of the Beauforts clearly shows that they had no legitimist title to the throne, that of the House of York as clearly tells their priority over all the other surviving descendants of Edward III, including the reigning King Henry VI.

Richard Plantagenet, Duke of York, in practice only used the arms of his grandfather, Edmund Langley: France and England quarterly with a silver label with three red roundels on each point. But by maternal descent he was entitled to quarter the arms of Lionel, Duke of Clarence, together with the arms of Mortimer and Ulster, the possession of which, as shown above, had become the heraldic criterion of legitimism; the title *de jure* to the throne having passed, at the

K

failure of the Black Prince's line, to the Mortimers descendant from Clarence, Edward III's next son.

It was objected against Richard when he claimed the throne that he did not bear the Clarence arms, " but he answered thereunto that he might lawfully have done it," wrote Camden, " but forbare it for a time, as he did for making his claim to the throne."

Therefore when Richard laid before the Lords a pedigree showing that in strict hereditary right he had a better claim to the throne than the reigning king, and ought not merely to succeed him but to replace him, they could only admit the justice of his claim. But while recognising Richard as the heir, they declined to depose Henry.

To sum up the conclusions of a rather involved chapter :

(i) The right to bear the arms of Lionel, Duke of Clarence, quartered with those of Mortimer and Ulster, indicated a right to the throne on legitimist grounds. Richard Plantagenet was entitled to these arms (Table V).

(ii) The white rose, probably derived from the Mortimers, was a legitimist emblem, and as such was used by Richard to symbolise his right to the throne.

(iii) The red rose, the emblem of the Lancastrian kings, represented a title to the throne based only on Parliamentary sanction (Table VI).

(iv) The arms of the Beauforts (whence sprang Henry VII) apparently confirm the intention that this family should be barred from the royal succession (Table VII).

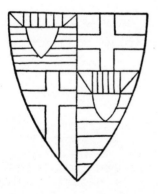

FIG. 140.—MORTIMER AND ULSTER QUARTERLY :
Arms used by Edmund, Earl of March, legitimist heir to Richard II.

FIG. 141.—The Bear and Ragged Staff.

XIV

THE WARS OF THE ROSES

" This here ought to have been a red rose tree, and we put in a white one
by mistake ; and if the Queen was to find it out, we should all have our heads
cut off, you know."—*Alice in Wonderland.*

THE roses first came to blows in 1455, when York, dismissed from
the Protectorship which he had held during Henry VI's temporary
insanity, gathered his allies to resist Somerset's restoration to power.
Foremost among his adherents were the Nevilles, father and son,
respectively Earls of Salisbury and Warwick.

The great House of Neville was typical of many lesser families
in that, like the Royal House itself, it was split in two by the divergent
sympathies and ambitions of its members.   At its head was the Earl
of Westmoreland, whose descendants by his first wife—a Stafford—
adhered to the Lancastrian cause, and a branch of the family, now
represented by Lord Abergavenny, added a red rose to their arms.
But the junior line of Nevilles, although closely allied to the House
of Lancaster through Westmoreland's second wife, Joane Beaufort,
turned from the red rose to the white because Cicely Neville, called
" the White Rose of Raby," sister to Salisbury and aunt of Warwick,
was married to the Duke of York, and might therefore become Queen
of England.

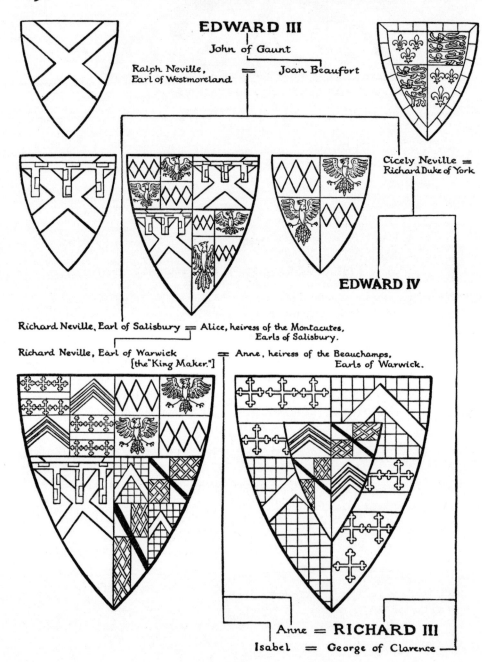

EDWARD III

John of Gaunt

Ralph Neville,   =   Joan Beaufort
Earl of Westmoreland

Cicely Neville   =
Richard Duke of York

EDWARD IV

Richard Neville, Earl of Salisbury = Alice, heiress of the Montacutes,
                                          Earls of Salisbury.

Richard Neville, Earl of Warwick == Anne, heiress of the Beauchamps,
[the "King Maker."]   Earls of Warwick.

Anne = RICHARD III

Isabel = George of Clarence

TABLE VIII.—THE RISE OF THE KING-MAKER.

The heraldry of the Yorkist Nevilles is interesting but curiously misleading. Richard Neville the elder had differenced his paternal arms—a silver saltire on red—by a label of the Lancastrian colours, white and blue, denoting his mother's family; with the anomalous result that the chief supporters of the House of York, including the King-maker himself, carried a definitely Lancastrian emblem in their arms.

The foregoing table shows how the two Nevilles acquired their quarterings, which clearly reflected the extent of their power and possessions. The elder, having gained the earldom of Salisbury by marriage with the heiress of the Montacutes, assumed their arms (which included those of the Monthermers), giving them precedence before his paternal coat. This complete shield became the armorial inheritance of his son, who, by marrying the heiress of the Beauchamps (themselves blood representatives of the Newburghs, Clares and Despencers), acquired the earldom of Warwick, and added the appropriate quarterings to his own, thus building up the following arms :

Grand
Quarterings. Quartered :

I.	1 and 4.	A gold fess and six crosslets on red, for *Beauchamp*.
	2 and 3.	Three red chevrons on gold, for *Clare*.
II.	1 and 4.	Three red fusils on silver, for *Montacute*.[1]
	2 and 3.	A green eagle on gold, for *Monthermer*.
III.		*Neville* (described above).
IV.	1 and 4.	Gold and blue chequers and an ermine chevron, for *Newburgh*, former Earls of Warwick.
	2 and 3.	Silver and red quarters, on the red pieces gold frets, and over all a black bend, for *Despencer*.

The Bear and the Ragged Staff.

His marriage brought the King-maker not only the earldom of Warwick but also its two famous badges, " the rampant bear chained to the ragged staff " (Fig. 141). Tradition says these were the emblems of the Earls of Warwick in Saxon times, and even that they date from

---

[1] A good instance of the more obscure kind of heraldic pun. Each fusil represents a *mont acute*.

King Arthur's days, commemorating the exploits of remote and mythical earls. But history only knows them as the badges of the Beauchamps and their successors in the earldom, and as such, together and separately, the Bear and the Ragged Staff were familiar emblems in fifteenth-century England. To-day they survive as a common inn-sign.

Shakespeare, who seems to have regarded the bear as the emblem of Salisbury as well as of Warwick, makes memorable reference to it when he puts these words into the mouth of York :

> *" York.*   Call hither to the stake my two brave bears,
> That with the very shaking of their chains
> They may astonish these fell lurking curs.
> Bid Salisbury and Warwick come to me.
>
> *Warwick and Salisbury enter.*
>
> *Clifford.*   Are these thy bears ?   We'll bait thy bears to death,
> And manacle the bearward in their chains,
> If thou darest bring them to the baiting place."

And later old Clifford threatens Warwick thus :

> " From thy burgonet I will rend thy bear,
> And tread it under foot with all contempt,
> Despite the bearward that protects the bear."

Queen Margaret and the White Swan.

York and his bear marched on London, and met the royal troops at St. Albans, where Somerset was killed. The leadership of the Lancastrian faction was then undertaken by Queen Margaret, anxious to secure the throne for her infant son. Margaret bore the arms of her father, René, the impoverished Duke of Anjou, titular King of Jerusalem and Sicily, which are still in use by Queens' College, Cambridge (Fig. 144). The quarterings are : (i) Hungary, (ii) Naples, (iii) Jerusalem, (iv) Anjou, (v) Bar, (vi) Lorraine. (The border, which is of green, has been added by the College.)

There followed an interval of peace, during which Margaret sought to win support for the Lancastrian cause. She travelled up

Fig. 142.—Ludlow.   Fig. 143.—Rivers.

Yorkist Roses.

and down the country, undertaking a sort of election campaign, and distributing to all who would wear it her son's badge, the white swan of Bohun.

The war was renewed in 1459, when York, Salisbury and Warwick assembled at Ludlow. The arms of that town commemorate its Yorkist associations. They consist of a white lion " couchant guardant " (the lion of March) between three roses of York on blue (Fig. 142). The King himself took the field, defeated the Yorkists, and drove the leaders overseas. They returned in the following year, and in rapid succession befell the Yorkist victory at Northampton and the Lancastrian counter-victory at Wakefield. Here the Duke of York was killed, and his head, derisively crowned with paper, was set up over the gate of York with that of the Earl of Salisbury and other lords.

The White Rose in the Sun.

The new Yorkist leader was Richard's son, Edward, Earl of March, who, having defeated the Lancastrians at Mortimer's Cross in Herefordshire, was crowned at London, and pursued Queen Margaret's army northward to Towton. Of the bloody battle fought on the banks of the little river Cock, where thousands of Lancastrians perished, we have heraldic record in the crest of the Yorkshire family of Hildyard— a cock, in memory of an ancestor who fell by that stream on the side

of the red rose; and in the word " Towton " accompanying the
crest of the Mathews of Llandaff, recalling the tradition that Sir
David Mathew was Edward's standard-bearer at that battle.

Edward IV, whose reign thus bloodily began, signalised the triumph
of the white rose by superimposing it on the sun, the badge York had
inherited from Richard II, to which Shakespeare refers :

> " Now is the winter of our discontent
> Made glorious summer by this sun of York."

Thus was formed the famous badge known as the " white rose-en-
soleil."

Holinshed tells us that before the battle of Mortimer's Cross,
Edward saw the sun " like three sunnes, and suddenlie ioined
altogither in one ; at which sight he took such courage that he, fiercelie
setting on his enimies, put them to flight ; and for this cause men
imagined that he gave the sunne in his full brightnesse for his badge
or cognisance." The phenomenon is not unknown, but cannot be
accepted as having given rise to a badge which was obviously inherited.

Several families that have white roses in their arms claim that
they denote adherence to the Yorkist cause. An authentic instance
is provided by the coat of augmentation granted to Sir Bartholomew
Rivers, a staunch Yorkist. It had a blue field with a silver engrailed
fesse charged with a plain red one, and thereon three white roses, the
fesse being placed between three white swans, referring indirectly to
the name Rivers (Fig. 143).

The Falcon Released.

Edward IV now commanded his son, the new Duke of York,
to bear the fetterlock about his falcon open, in token that the line
was no longer locked away from the throne as it had been when old
Edmund Langley bore the falcon and fetterlock.

To-day the Yorkist fetterlock encircles the Lancastrian rose in the
shield of Bewdley, Worcestershire, an old Mortimer manor which
passed into the hands of the Crown at Edward IV's accession.

Elizabeth Woodville.

Edward IV bore the Lancastrian rose no ill; he even anticipated the Tudor rose by producing a combination of the red and white flowers. This harmonises with the meaning we have attached to the red rose, regarding it as the symbol of Parliamentary sanction, for Edward's claim to the throne " was declared to be by two maner of waies," wrote Holinshed; " the first, as sonne and heire to duke Richard his father, right inheritor to the same; the second, by authoritie of parlement, and forfeiture committed by king Henrie."

But Edward's union of the roses by no means reflected the state of the realm. Rather it symbolised the state of the King's heart, for he had somewhat indiscreetly fallen before the charms of Elizabeth Woodville, the daughter of one prominent Lancastrian and the widow of another.

This lady bore an elaborate shield of six quarterings, five being derived from the arms of her aristocratic mother, Jacquetta de Luxembourg (who quartered the arms of Luxembourg, Baux, Cyprus, Orsini and St. Paul), and the sixth quartering containing the arms of Woodville, a red cantoned fesse on silver (Fig. 145). Elizabeth Woodville augmented the College which her predecessor, Queen Margaret, had founded at Cambridge, and Queens' College therefore possesses these arms, though it rarely uses them.

Last Battles of the Roses.

King-making Warwick viewed with suspicion the favours showered on the Woodvilles and their Lancastrian friends, and when Edward made it clear that he was determined to humble the over-mighty earl, the bear and ragged staff joined the black bull of Clarence, the King's brother, and forsook the white rose for the red. Edward was forced to flee the country, and Henry VI was set on the throne again.

Then in 1471 Edward returned and marched on London. He met Warwick at Barnet. That day the white rose-en-soleil, which was worn as a badge by Edward's troops, served him well. On Warwick's side was De Vere, whose men were wearing the silver star of crusading

FIG. 144.—QUEEN MARGARET OF ANJOU.   FIG. 145.—QUEEN ELIZABETH WOODVILLE.

Founders of Queens' College, Cambridge.

FIG. 146.—WILLIAM OF WYKEHAM,
*Founder of Winchester College and New College,
Oxford.*

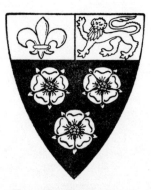

FIG. 147.—ETON COLLEGE.   FIG. 148.—KING'S COLLEGE,   FIG. 149.—CLOOS.
                                          CAMBRIDGE.

memories (Chapter VI). Warwick, seeing through a mist the star of de Vere, mistook it for Edward's shining rose, and charged—against his own supporters. During the confusion the Earl of Oxford fled, Warwick was slain and the battle was lost. Thereafter befell Tewkesbury, the murder of Henry VI and the destruction of the House of Lancaster.

Drayton, in *Polyolbion*, tells the incident thus :—

" The envious mist so much deceived their sight,
  That where eight hundred men, which valiant Oxford brought,
  Wore comets on their coats, great Warwick's force, which thought
  They had King Edward's been, which so with suns were drest,
  First made their shot at them, who, by their friends distrest,
  Constrained were to fly, being scatter'd here and there."

Educational Foundations.

King Henry VI's characteristic and most enduring memorials, his allied educational foundations at Eton and Cambridge, proclaim their royal origin and their kinship by their heraldry. To " the College of the Blessed Mary of Eton beside Windsor " he gave for arms three white lilies (emblematic of the Virgin) on black, and on a chief divided into blue and red compartments a gold fleur-de-lys and lion from the Royal Arms (Fig. 147).

To King's College, Cambridge, a similar shield was granted, white roses being given instead of lilies (Fig. 148). According to the grant of arms, the black field signified the perpetuity of the foundation " for ages to come " ; the roses express the hope that it may " bring forth the rightest flowers redolent in every kind of knowledge " ; and the fleur-de-lys and lion are intended to " impart something of kingly nobility to declare the work truly regal and famous."

To his clerk, Nicholas Cloos, for services in connection with King's College, Henry granted a white shield with a black chevron and chief, with three lilies on the chevron, and three roses on the chief (Fig. 149).

In his deliberate destruction of the House of Lancaster, Edward omitted two members—the Lady Margaret Beaufort, the Duke of

Somerset's daughter, now married to the Yorkist Lord Stanley, and her son (by her former marriage with Owen Tudor), Henry of Richmond. The latter had been sent for safety overseas, and his existence did not trouble Edward IV.

Like her kinsman, Henry VI, Lady Margaret Beaufort is commemorated by two great houses of learning, Christ's and St. John's Colleges, Cambridge. Both bear the Beaufort arms, which are carved over their gates complete with supporters—the Lancastrian antelopes, or yales—and the eagle crest of the Beauforts, and flanked by badges—the Lancastrian rose and the Beaufort portcullis.

New College, Oxford, and Winchester College both bear the arms of William of Wykeham, their founder—two black chevrons and three red roses (not the Lancastrian flowers) on white (Fig. 146). Some writers have thought the chevron to represent the gable end of a house, and applying this rather fanciful theory to Wykeham's shield we find it suggests his most permanent labours as the architect of two houses of learning.

The White Boar.

The " sun of York " set in 1483, when the death of Edward IV was quickly succeeded by the murder of his little son Edward V and the seizure of the throne by Richard of Gloucester.

Richard III's famous badge was a silver boar (Fig. 150), of which no explanation is forthcoming except Planché's tentative suggestion that it was a pun on the name " Ebor "; against this we may argue that Richard never held the honour of York, and that those who did so did not use the boar as a badge. If a pun theory be required, we may suggest that the royal title *Rex Anglie* suggested *sanglier*, the heraldic term for boar; but Richard III seems to have used the boar badge before he became king.

If Richard was the crooked creature that tradition represents him, it may be that he was driven by his deformed figure and twisted character to a kind of defiant cynicism which led him to adopt as a badge the animal which he knew himself to resemble, but it seems very doubtful whether he was the monster that the writers of Tudor times made him.

FIG. 150.—BADGE OF RICHARD III.

Shakespeare referred to Richard III by his favourite emblem when he wrote:

> " The wretched, bloody and usurping boar
> That spoilt your summer fields and fruitful vines,
> Swills your warm blood like wash, and makes his trough
> In your embowelled bosoms, this foul swine
> Lies even now in the centre of this isle."

And again :

> " Thou elvish-marked, abortive, rooting hog."

When Richard's career of murder and oppression fanned the embers of treason and rebellion, this jingle ran about the land :

> " The Cat, the Rat, and Lovel our Dog
> Rule all England under a Hog."

The Cat and the Rat were Sir William Catesby and Sir Richard Ratcliffe, Lord Lovel's badge was a Dog, and the Hog was of course the King. The author of this rhyme, one Collingbourne of Wiltshire, paid for it with his life.

Readers of Holinshed may recall his anecdote of Lord Stanley's ominous dream before Lord Hastings's sudden seizure and execution. Stanley dreamed that " a boare with his tuskes so rased them (him and Hastings) both by the heads that the bloud ran about both their shoulders. And forasmuch as the protector (Richard) gave the boare for his cognisance, this dreame made so fearfull an impression " on Stanley, that he sent to Hastings proposing instant flight. Hastings replied that if they fled, " then had the boare a cause likelie to rase us with his tuskes, as folk that fled for some falsehood." Disregarding the omen, next day he suffered its fulfilment.

FIG. 151.—GLOUCESTER.   FIG. 152.—QUEENS' COLLEGE,
                                          CAMBRIDGE.

The head of Richard's boar between a red and a white rose, each halved with a sun, appears on gold and purple in the chief of the shield of Gloucester, Richard's duchy.   Below are the civic sword and the sword-bearer's hat on a gold pale between gold horseshoes and nails on green (Fig. 151).   The boar's head also appears in a shield used by Queens' College, Cambridge, together with the cross of St. Margaret and the crosier of St. Bernard (Fig. 152).

The Crowned Hawthorn.

The opposition to Richard centred on the last of the Beauforts and the first of the royal Tudors, young Henry of Richmond, who hunted the kingly boar on Bosworth Field.   Richard was slain, and his crown was found under a hawthorn bush, and placed on Henry's head by Lord Stanley (afterwards first Earl of Derby).   In memory of this dramatic and joyful end to the battle, Henry VII took the hawthorn bush, surmounted by a crown, as a badge, and it was to be seen in stained glass in his chapel at Westminster (Fig. 153). The window was destroyed during the Second World War.

An interesting story of Bosworth is told by the family of Cheney to account for a feature of their arms, which consist of six silver lions rampant on blue [1] with an ermine canton charged with a bull's scalp and horns.   Burke relates that " Sir John Cheney, of Shirland, an eminent soldier under the banner of the Earl of Richmond at Bosworth, personally encountering King Richard, was felled to the ground by the monarch, had his crest struck off and his head laid bare ; for some time, it is said, he remained stunned, but recovering after a while, he cut the skull and horns off the hide of an ox which chanced to be near, and fixed them upon his head to supply the loss of the upper part of his helmet ; he then returned to the field of battle, and did such signal service that Henry, on being proclaimed King, assigned Cheney for crest the ' bull's cap ' which his descendants still bear."   The bull's cap is now incorporated in the arms (Fig. 154).

After Bosworth " the proud and bragging white boar was violently rased and pulled down from every sign and place where it might be spied."

[1] Feudal arms based on those of William Longuespee, a descendant of Henry I ; see Chapter V.

FIG. 153.—THE CROWNED HAWTHORN.   FIG. 154.—CHENEY.

Memorials of Bosworth.

FIG. 155.—HENRY VII AND ELIZABETH OF YORK.

XV

UNDER THE TUDOR ROSE

" We will unite the white rose and the red ;
Smile Heaven upon this fair conjunction
That long have frowned upon their enmity."

Shakespeare, *Richard III.*

HENRY VII's accession, while it ended the long anarchy of the Wars of the Roses, cannot be regarded as the ultimate victory of the red rose. It is true that Henry mounted the throne with that Parliamentary sanction for which, viewed historically, the red rose stood ; but having gained recognition as king in his own right, he wisely satisfied the claims of legitimism by marrying the heiress of the white rose, Elizabeth of York, thus ensuring that his descendants' title to the throne should be unquestionable.

On his marriage, therefore, the Royal Arms were at length borne upon one shield with the arms of Mortimer and Ulster, which at the outset of the Wars of the Roses had represented the legitimist cause, and now formed part of the arms of Elizabeth of York (Fig. 155). Elizabeth, as a daughter of Edward IV, also bore the Royal Arms, so in the combined arms of Henry and his wife they appeared twice.

144

The Tudor Rose.

As in his arms, so in his badges Henry expressed the reconciliation of the Parliamentary and legitimist principles, for he united the rival roses themselves in the beautiful emblem which is known as the Tudor Rose. This rose was variously represented as divided vertically or quarterly red and white, or as a red rose with a white one super-imposed on it (Fig. 156). The last is the most usual form, and repre-sents the application to a badge of the heraldic rule that when a man marries an heiress of another family he places her arms on an inescut-cheon in the centre of his own shield.

How the Tudor rose appealed to the imagination of the people is shown by verses called, " A Crowne-garland of Golden Roses gathered out of England's loyal garden : a princely song made of the

FIG. 156.—TUDOR ROSES.

red rose and white, royally united together by King Henry VII and Elizabeth Plantagenet." One stanza will suffice :

" These roses sprang and budded faire, and carried such a grace,
That Kings of England in their armes afford them worthy place,
And flourish may these roses long that all the world may tell
The owners of these princely flowers in virtues doe excell."

Henry incorporated the Tudor rose in a collar, with a pendant of St. George and the Dragon, which he gave as insignia to the Order of the Garter, and it became customary to surround the Royal Arms with it (Fig. 157).

In introducing St. George and the Dragon, Henry had, of course,
L

FIG. 157.—ARMS OF HENRY VII, *with the Collar of the Garter.*

no thought or knowledge of the emblem's ancient association with the eternal warfare between the sun and darkness; but to us who, taking an historical view, notice this innovation in our national heraldry in his reign, the saint appears as the champion of ordered government striking down the monster of anarchy.

Under the red rose, " constitutional progress had outrun administrative order " (Stubbs), and the Tudor rose became the symbol of a strong personal rule which so disciplined the nation as to fit it for the gradual development of self-government in succeeding centuries.

Decline of Feudal Badges.

Henry's first task was to ensure against any recurrence of lawless violence between political factions. Realising that the maintenance by great lords of private armies of liveried retainers was a menace to the royal power and the peace of the realm, he vigorously prosecuted the policy, vainly attempted by some of his predecessors, of suppressing livery and maintenance. One result was that heraldic badges, which had been so prominent during the factious fifteenth century, fell into desuetude as emblems of political significance, but lingered on as mere decorations.

At the same time Henry prohibited the use of family cries in battle, thinking that the war-cries with which the fields of Wakefield and Towton had resounded were too apt to recall bitter memories, and to prolong feuds which were better forgotten. He decreed that in future all men should call on the national patron, St. George.

But his measures to secure internal peace could not be entirely peaceful. He had to crush implacable Yorkists who so far mistook the tenor of the times as to think that rebellion might still be a profitable business, and he took the opportunity of pruning the white rose tree of a blossom in the person of Edward of Warwick, who had the proud but highly dangerous distinction of being the last heir-male of the Plantagenets.

Tudor Badges.

Henry VII used as badges many of the emblems which we have noticed in previous chapters, to imply that he was the representative of the several royal lines to which these badges belonged. In addition to the crowned hawthorn, memorial of Bosworth, and the Tudor rose, he used the fleur-de-lys of Edward III, the sunburst of Richard II, and the falcon and fetterlock of the House of York. As denoting his immediate ancestors, he displayed the red dragon of Cadwallader (from whom the Tudors claimed descent) placed on the Tudor colours white and green; and the Beaufort portcullis (Fig. 158).

From Henry's partiality to the portcullis, and the fact that it was sometimes accompanied by the motto, *Altera Securitas,* an ingenious writer has imagined the portcullis to have been originally a punning device of the Tudors, the motto being very freely translated as " Two Door." The old heralds were guilty of many bad puns, but of this one they may be honourably acquitted, for the portcullis was a Beaufort badge before the marriage of Lady Margaret Beaufort with Edmund Tudor.

As supporters, Henry VII used variously a red dragon and white greyhound, two greyhounds, and a golden lion and red dragon.

The fortune amassed by Henry VII laid the foundation of his son's despotism, and it is significant that he valued the services of his cofferer, William Cope, so highly as to give him arms displaying the royal favour, a white shield with three red roses, and three fleurs-de-lys on a blue chevron (Fig. 159).

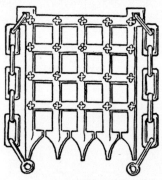

FIG. 158.—THE PORTCULLIS.

FIG. 159.—COPE.

FIG. 160.—UNITED BADGES OF HENRY VIII AND CATHERINE OF ARAGON.

Henry VIII.

But for the introduction of a new supporter, a silver cock (*gallus*) to stand for Wales (*Galles*) Henry VIII made no change in the Royal Arms, though his matrimonial adventures caused them to be marshalled with many different coats during his reign.

At Henry's accession, his lions and lilies stood beside the elaborate heraldic display of Catherine of Aragon ; and he also united the badges of England and Spain, joining his Tudor rose sometimes to a bundle of arrows, for Aragon, and sometimes, with extraordinary botanical effect, to the pomegranate of Granada (Fig. 160).

Arms and badges tell how at the outset of his reign he was attracted towards the Spanish Royal House by both personal and political influences.

Not for nothing did Henry retain in his arms the French fleurs-de-lys. Young, ambitious and with full coffers to back him, he determined to prosecute his ancestral claims, and he joined his father-in-law of Spain, the Pope and the Emperor Maximilian against France.

It was during this period of alliance with the Papacy that he received the title, *Fidei Defensor*, which his Protestant successors retain.

Henry's victory over the French army, which on account of the enemy's speedy flight the English called " the Battle of the Spurs," has heraldic record in the shield of the family of Clerk. Sir John Clerk

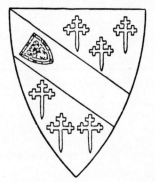

FIG. 161.—CLERK : *the Battle*   FIG. 162.—HOWARD, *with the augmentation granted for the*
of the Spurs.   *victory at Flodden.*

bore for arms a red bend and three black roundels on silver, with three
golden swans on the bend.   At this battle he captured the royal Duke
de Longueville, and was permitted to add to his shield a blue canton
(on the sinister side) charged with a silver half-ram (the Duke's
supporter, suitably bisected) and two fleurs-de-lys with a silver baton
sinister across them (Fig. 161).

Henry VIII's retention of the fleurs-de-lys is the subject of a story
which may have more point than truth.   It is told that one day he
greeted Lord Abergavenny, who had parted with his patrimony, with
the words, " Good-morrow, my lord Burgenny—without Burgenny."
To which Abergavenny replied, " Good-morrow, my liege lord of
France—without France."

Flodden.

Meanwhile James IV of Scotland, true to the policy which the
fleurs-de-lys in his arms proclaimed, had taken the occasion of Henry's
French campaign to invade Northumberland.   He was met by Thomas
Howard, Earl of Surrey, at Flodden.   Like Henry IV at Shrewsbury,
the Scottish King caused five of his knights to wear the royal coat-of-
arms.   This, being known to the Scots, led them to disbelieve the
news of their King's death.   It was none the less true.   With James

fell the flower of Scottish nobility, and Flodden ensured the quietness of the Scots for years.

To this day the arms of the Dukes of Norfolk tell of this victory. Before Flodden the Howard shield contained a silver bend and six crosslets, pointed at the foot, on red. To this, " that it may be known to all that (the victory) was achieved by the generalship, guidance and governance " of Surrey, was added on the bend an escutcheon of the arms of Scotland, with but half the lion, and that pierced through the throat by an arrow (Fig. 162). The last detail refers to the fact that King James's body was found pierced by arrows.

According to Holinshed, " Thomas Howard, Earl of Surrie, gave to his servants as a note of this conquest this cognisance (to wear on the left arm), a white lion (the beast which he before bare as the proper ensign of that house) standing over a red lion (the peculiar note of the kingdom of Scotland), and tearing the same red lion with his pawes."

Some years later an augmentation was granted to Thomas Wharton, Governor of Carlisle, for his services in the Scottish wars, especially at the battle of Solway Ness. To his arms, a white maunch (lady's sleeve) on black, was added a gold engrailed border charged with eight

FIG. 163.—WHARTON :
the Battle of Solway Ness.

FIG. 164.—FARQUHARSON :
the Battle of Pinkie.

crossed pairs of lions' paws—the paws torn from the Scottish lion (Fig. 163). At the same time he was given as a supporter a red lion fretted with gold—possibly intended to represent the Scottish lion caught in a net. Probably there is a suggestion of the Franco-Scottish pact in a device of James V of Scotland of a whale led by a little fish —Pliny's *musculus* and Kipling's " small 'stute fish "—with the motto, " He urges on a greater "; as though to suggest that Scotland's policy was to direct the power of France against their common enemy, England.

There is a reference to the battle of Pinkie, 1547 (when Somerset was victorious over the Scots), in the arms of the family of Farquharson, who commemorate the death of their ancestor, Finlay Mor, the Scottish standard-bearer. The significant quartering is of silver, and contains a fir tree, with the Scottish banner on a red chief, and a dagger on a silver canton (Fig. 164). The dagger is the weapon with which another ancestor killed a rebel Cumming.

Wolsey and Cromwell.

Thomas Wolsey, the son of an Ipswich butcher, whom Henry raised up to be his minister, possessed no paternal arms, but he adopted a shield which is an interesting example of heraldic piracy (Fig. 165).

As a Suffolk man he placed on his black shield a silver engrailed cross taken from the arms of the Uffords, anciently earls of Suffolk. Thereon he set four blue leopards' faces, probably suggested by the bearings of the De la Poles, also earls of Suffolk. Wolsey had no connection with either of these families.

In the centre of the cross he placed a red lion passant guardant, probably alluding to Pope Leo X from whom Wolsey received his Cardinal's hat; and he added a golden chief containing a red rose, symbolic of his position as a royal minister, and two black Cornish choughs, taken from the arms of his sainted namesake, Thomas Becket.

Some may think that these arms reflect the pretentious character of Wolsey, who lacked the innate gentility which scruples to assume marks of honour belonging to others. But the main point of historic

FIG. 165.—CARDINAL WOLSEY, AND CHRIST CHURCH, OXFORD.

FIG. 166.—READING UNIVERSITY.

interest in the shield is that it contains both royal and ecclesiastical emblems, thus reflecting Wolsey's position as both Chancellor and Cardinal, which enabled him to gather into his capable hands all the civil and religious authority of the realm, and so prepare the way for the personal despotism of Henry VIII.

Incidentally, in their elaboration these arms presage the coming decline in the art of heraldry.

Wolsey's arms are borne to-day by Christ Church, Oxford (formerly Cardinal College), and Portsmouth Grammar School. Reading University has a shield which refers to both Christ Church and Reading Abbey, the upper part of the shield containing three gold scallops on red for the Abbey, and the lower part a silver engrailed cross, charged with a red rose, on black, for the College, which was concerned in its foundation (Fig. 166).

Wolsey's enemies assigned him other arms than those of his own choice. A poem by William Roy, Tyndale's assistant in the translation of the Bible, directed against the Cardinal, was prefaced by an armorial frontispiece whereon appeared a fictitious coat-of-arms consisting of six red axes on black. These, to coin a phrase, may be called " arms of derision." Beneath the drawing appeared these lines :

FIG. 167.—BUCKINGHAM :
*Civic arms derived from the
badge of the Earls.*

FIG. 168.—THOMAS CROMWELL.

FIG. 169.—SEE OF
CHICHESTER.

" Of the proud Cardinal this is the shield,
    Borne up between two angels of Satan.
    The six bloody axes in a bare field
    Sheweth the cruelty of the red man
    Who hath devoured the beautiful swan ;
    Mortal enemy of the white lion ;
    Carter of York, the vile butcher's son."

This verse refers to the persecution of the great families which by
blood stood near to the throne. The " beautiful swan " was the
Duke of Buckingham (whose ancestor derived the badge from the
Bohuns—Chapter VII), and the " white lion " was the Duke of
Norfolk.

In 1521 Edward Stafford, third Duke of Buckingham, was charged
with treason on the grounds that he aspired to the crown, and was
executed. Any claim he might have made would have been absurdly
weak, and there is little doubt the accusation was engineered by
Wolsey to satisfy a personal grudge. A motto was one of the counts
against Buckingham in the chain of evidence forged to prove his intention of wearing the crown ; it was but the one word *Dorsenavant,*
" Henceforward," but it was twisted by the Buzfuz of the period into a
more powerful weapon than the " Chops and tomato sauce " which
was Mr. Pickwick's undoing.

" It was a great pity that so fair and goodly a Buck should be worried to death by a butcher's curr," said the Emperor Charles V, according to Camden; " alluding either to the name Buckingham, or to a Buck, which was a badge of honour to that family."

When Wolsey fell he was succeeded by his creature, Thomas Cromwell, the son, it is said, of a Putney blacksmith, and not related to the old baronial family of Cromwell. He took as his arms three gold lions on blue (perhaps suggested by a single silver lion on blue borne by a fourteenth-century Cromwell), and added a fesse which was identical with the chief in Wolsey's arms, from which it was, of course, taken (Fig. 168).

Thus the Cornish choughs from Thomas Becket's shield passed into the arms of the very man at whose instigation Becket's shrine at Canterbury was demolished, and the sainted archbishop's bones violated as those of a traitor to his king. Cromwell could have known nothing of the historical associations of the emblems he displayed, or he could not with consistency have continued to bear them.

An indirect reference to the iconoclastic period of the Reformation is found in the blazon (description in heraldic terms) of the arms of the See of Chichester. The shield is blue, with a white-robed figure seated on a throne. From the mouth issues a sword (Fig. 169). The last detail alone, having regard to St. John's words, " and out of His mouth goeth a sharp sword," identifies the figure as the Almighty; yet the arms were till recently described in some peerages as " a Prester John sitting on a tombstone."

It is probable that the Sussex bishops, fearing that their arms might be held to be idolatrous, chose to disguise their sacred character rather than abandon them, and deliberately invoked Prester John, the mythical priest-king of mediæval Asia, to throw dust in the eyes of prying Protestant fanatics.

Henry's Queens.

Aided by Cromwell, Henry repudiated Catherine of Aragon and raised up Anne Boleyn in her place. Anne was entitled to the simple arms of her father, a red chevron and three black bulls' heads allusive

FIG. 170.—JANE SEYMOUR.   FIG. 171.—CATHERINE HOWARD.   FIG. 172.—KATHERINE PARR.

Heraldic Honours of Henry VIII's Queens.

to the name Boleyn or Bullen, with the quarterings of other gentle but inconspicuous families. Henry seems to have thought that these arms, displayed beside the royal lilies and lions, would remind people too forcibly of the comparative lowliness of his new Queen's birth, and occasion such comments as Shakespeare attributes to Wolsey : " The late Queen's gentlewoman, a knight's daughter, to be her mistress's mistress." So when he made her Marchioness of Pembroke, as a prelude to raising her to the throne, he caused her to abandon the arms of Boleyn in favour of a proud shield containing quarterings of Lancaster, Angoulême, Guienne, Butler, Rochfort, Brotherton and Warrenne. To the first three of these Anne had no hereditary right, and the others she bore only by waiving heraldic rules.

Queen Catherine's badges, her native pomegranate and arrow joined severally with the Tudor rose, continued after the dissolution of the marriage they symbolised, and stood as a mute protest against the divorce. They therefore became emblems of English Catholicism, being borne by Queen Mary, a Catholic no less by personal interest than by religious conviction, since to accept the Reformation would be to admit herself illegitimate.

On the other hand, the badge adopted by Anne Boleyn, a silver falcon holding a sceptre, became an emblem of Protestantism, and was inherited by Queen Elizabeth, the child of the Reformation as Mary was of the old faith.

To the family of Jane Seymour, who succeeded Anne Boleyn, Henry granted a shield of honour made up of emblems from the Royal Arms, the lions being placed on a red pile, with three blue fleurs-de-lys on gold on each side (Fig. 170). This is still quartered with the Seymour arms, two golden wings joined together on red. The Seymours remember the Queen of their name and her son, Edward VI, by bearing as their crest a phœnix in flames, which was devised by Henry VIII as a fitting emblem of his wife who gave her life in giving him a son.

Catherine Howard seems to have been doubly beloved by Henry VIII, for he gave her two shields of honour to quarter with the proud arms of Howard. One was of blue, with three gold fleurs-de-lys and two ermine " flanches " (curved side pieces), each bearing a red rose (Fig. 171). The other was blue with two gold lions and four half fleurs-de-lys.

Katherine Parr also received heraldic honours, a gold shield with a red pile between six red roses, and three white ones on the pile. This she bore with her paternal coat of two blue bars on silver within a black engrailed border (Fig. 172).

The Irish Harp.

Henry VIII, whose vigorous suppression of the FitzGerald insurrection paved the way for Elizabeth's conquest of Ireland, was the first monarch in modern times to use the harp as a royal Irish emblem. Some doubt existed as to the true arms of Ireland. In Edward IV's reign a commission appointed to discover them reported in favour of the three gold crowns on blue, from the banner of St. Edmund borne by the Anglo-Norman invaders. Edward IV accordingly placed these crowns palewise on his Irish groat (Fig. 173).

The three crowns cannot have been merely overlooked by Henry VIII; he must have had some reason for abandoning them in favour of the harp, and that reason was probably his adoption of a new royal style. Edward IV had been content to call himself *Dominus Hibernie ;*

Henry VIII thought fit to become *Rex,* and the inscription on the harp side of his Irish groat (Fig. 174) is the second half of HENRIC. 8. D: G: ANGL. FRANC. W: ET HIBERNIE REX: 38:

FIG. 173.—THE THREE CROWNS.   FIG. 174.—THE HARP.

Irish Coins.

On assuming the title of King of Ireland, Henry naturally wished to celebrate it in his heraldry, and how better could he do so than by placing on his coins and using as a royal badge the ancient harp?

> " The harp that once through Tara's halls
> The soul of music shed."

The adoption of this famous emblem may perhaps have meant that Henry wished to be regarded as a successor to the old kings of Ireland, and sought to appeal to Irish nationalism. Tradition says that the very harp of Tara was in his possession, having been given him by the Pope.

A secondary reason suggested for the abandonment of the three crowns is, that arranged one above the other as on the coins they might be mistaken for the Papal tiara—a symbol which Henry could not brook after he had declared himself to be, " under Christ, supreme head on earth of the Church of England and Ireland."

The present arms and crest of Ireland are shown in Fig. 135.

Catholic Risings.

A banner displaying the Cross and Five Wounds of Christ became a sign of Catholicism in this and Elizabeth's reign. It was raised by the Lincolnshire insurgents and the " Pilgrimage of Grace " in 1536, when the breach with Rome and the dissolution of the monasteries produced trouble in the north. One of the banners borne by the Lincolnshire men was thus described :

> " The meaning of the plough borne in the banner was to encourage the husbandmen. The meaning of the chalice and host was borne in remembrance that chalices, cross and jewels of the Church would be taken away. The meaning of the five wounds was to couraging of the people to fight in Christ's cause."

The Five Wounds were displayed again in 1569, when the sons of the " Pilgrims " took part in the Northern Rising. On this occasion the banner was entrusted to Richard Norton, as the ballad tells :

> " Erle Percy there his ancyent spred,
>   The Halfe-Moone shining all soe faire :
> The Nortons ancyent had the Crosse
>   And the Five Wounds our Lord did beare."

Henry took the occasion of the Pilgrimage of Grace to cut off some of the remaining heads of the *planta genista*, including Courtenay, Marquis of Exeter ; Pole, Lord Montagu ; and Margaret of Clarence.

Heraldic malpractices were partly responsible for the downfall of Henry, Earl of Surrey, whom, with his father, the Duke of Norfolk, Henry feared for Catholic sympathies. Surrey permitted private ambitions to find expression in his arms. Descended from Thomas de Brotherton, son of Edward I, the Howards quartered the English lions, differenced by a silver label. Their royal descent passed in three instances through women, and they could make no valid claim to the throne. But they seem to have contemplated securing the Regency at Henry's death, and it was suspected that Surrey aimed at marrying Princess Mary.

What chiefly betrayed Surrey was the manner in which he marshalled his heraldry. In the first place, he incorporated the arms of Edward the Confessor, granted by Richard II to Thomas Mowbray, Duke of Norfolk, but not to that nobleman's descendants. And in the second place, he removed the label from the quartering of Brotherton, thus bearing the royal lions without any differencing mark. (The illustration—Fig. 175—shows the relevant quarterings. In practice Surrey used others as well.)

The assumption that these changes in his arms were made by Surrey as a preliminary to taking steps towards the throne may not have been altogether unjustifiable, but as evidence of treason they were very weak, and his execution can only be regarded as typical of the political murders which marred Henry's later years.

The Catholic Restoration.

The reigns of Edward VI and Mary are heraldically not notable, though the arms of the former are still borne by many educational establishments which owe their foundation to him.

Mary's sincere Catholicism, which led to the temporary restoration of communion with Rome, is indicated by two of her devices. One represented Time raising up Truth from a pit, with the motto, *Veritas Temporis Filia.* The other is a sword upon an altar, with the legend, *Aræ et regni custodia.*

Her marriage with Philip II of Spain was indicated by the impaling of the English Royal Arms with those of Spain on our coinage. Philip assumed as a device Bellerophon fighting with a monster, expressive of his determination to fight heresy in England.

It is said that the crest of the family of Smijth, a salamander in flames (adopted in substitution of the old crest of an eagle holding an ostrich feather, denoting descent from the Black Prince), commemorates the escape from " Bloody Mary's " fires of Sir Thomas Smijth, a Secretary of State under Edward VI, who had been closely concerned with the advance of Protestantism.

FIG. 175.—HENRY, EARL OF SURREY : *The Arms which cost him his life.*

FIG. 176.—ROYAL ARMS OF ELIZABETH I

XVI

GLORIANA

"Thou sun, shine on her joyously; ye breezes, waft her wide;
 Our glorious SEMPER EADEM, the banner of our pride."
                                        Macaulay, *The Armada.*

PROCLAIMED by the title, "most worthy Empress from the Orcade
Islands to the Mountains Pyrenée," Elizabeth was unlikely to abate
her heraldic pretensions. Rather she sought to glorify her display
of arms by the lavish use of gold.

Whereas her predecessors had used a red mantling (the decorative
cloak falling about the shield), she adopted the gold mantling which,
with its ermine lining, adorns the Royal Arms to-day. She also
gilded the Welsh dragon, one of her supporters (Fig. 176). The
royal motto in her reign was *Semper Eadem*—"Always the Same."

Beside her mother's silver falcon, Elizabeth used as badges a
crowned rose with the inappropriate motto, *Rosa sine spina;* a sieve,
the significance of which has not been fathomed; and a phœnix,

M   161

FIG. 177.—MARY QUEEN OF SCOTS:
Maiden Arms.

FIG. 178.—ARMS AS WIFE OF THE
DAUPHIN OF FRANCE, *with
the inescutcheon of England
indicating pretensions to the
English throne.*

FIG. 179.—ARMS AFTER THE
DAUPHIN'S DEATH, *with
the half-inescutcheon of
England.*

ARMS OF MARY QUEEN OF SCOTS

popularly supposed to celebrate her recovery from small-pox. Placed on a medal, this emblem was accompanied by an inscription hailing the Queen as phœnix in all but death.

A bust of Elizabeth appeared in the arms she granted to Sir Thomas Weldon, Clerk of the Spicery. The honour is the more remarkable when we remember the strict supervision exercised over the portrayal of her royal features. The crest of the Virginia Merchants also represents Elizabeth, though the blazon sounds unflattering : " a maiden queen couped below the shoulders, her hair dishevelled."

The Succession Question.

" An expectant heir is like a coffin always in sight," said Elizabeth, and refused to consider who should succeed her. The problem was complicated by the religious position. Elizabeth's heir, by legitimist reckoning, was Mary, Queen of Scots, a Romanist who hated England, and was as unsuited an heir as she was eager. After her came Katherine Grey, sister to the unfortunate Lady Jane, and surviving descendant of Henry VII's younger daughter.

Both Mary and Katherine were entitled to include the royal lilies and lions in their shields. Mary did so without any differencing mark, but Katherine tactfully quartered not the actual Royal Arms, but those of the House of Beaufort with the distinctive blue and white border ; but this did not save her from prison.

Mary, Queen of Scots.

Though Elizabeth continued the old pretension to the throne of France by quartering the lilies in her shield, she was jealous that anyone should take similar liberties with her own arms, and their assumption by the Queen of Scots was a standing grievance.

As coheiress of the English Royal House (the male line having expired with Edward VI), Mary could claim to bear the English Royal Arms quarterly with those of Scotland (Fig. 177), and had she been content with this, Elizabeth would have had little cause to complain. But Mary carried her armorial pretensions further.

On her marriage with the Dauphin, the arms of Scotland were quartered with his (France and the Dauphiné quarterly), and regarding his wife as heir to the English throne he placed the Royal Arms of England in an " inescutcheon of pretence " (Fig. 178).

The Dauphin succeeded to the throne as Francis II. When he died, Mary, it seems, halved the shield illustrated in Fig. 178, and impaled the remnant with her maiden coat (Fig. 177), thus producing the elaborate shield which so offended Elizabeth (Fig. 179).

This method of marshalling arms was open to objection on technical heraldic grounds, and there is no doubt it was meant to emphasise Mary's claim to be Elizabeth's heiress. What puzzled the heralds (who do not seem to have worked out the above stages of Mary's armorial development) was the half-escutcheon of the English Royal Arms, " perhaps so given," wrote Strype, " to denote that another (and who should that be but Q. *Elizabeth* ?) had gotten Possession of the Crown in her Prejudice." And as if to confirm this interpretation, these lines were written under some paintings of the arms, one of which still hangs at Holyrood :

" The arms of MARY, Queen Dolphiness of *Fraunce*,
The Noblest Lady in Earth, for till advaunce ;
Of *Scotland* Queen, and of *England* also
Of *Fraunce*, as God hath providit so."

Mary's arms were delivered to the Earl Marshal of England and his heralds, who passed the following judgment on them :

" . . . we find the same prejudicial unto the Queen's Majesty [*i.e.* Elizabeth], her State and Dignity, and that hyt doth not appertain to any Foreign Prince, what Marriage soever he hath made with *England*, to quarter, bear or use the arms of England otherwise than in Pale [*i.e.* impaled] as in Token of marriage. And albeit *James* late Scottish King, Grandfather to the Scottish Queen, being but one of the collaterals, cannot, nor ought not to bear any Escutcheon of the Arms of *England* nor yet the Dolphin her Husband in the right of her, or otherwise."

The articles drawn up in 1572 against Mary, then detained in England, included this clause :

" Her claim to the Crown of *England* in Possession, with Refusal and Delay to remove the same ; Giving the arms of *England* without difference, in Escutcheons, Coat-arms, Plate, Alter-Cloaths, which were openly seen at the Triumph ; writing of the stile of *England, Scotland, France* and *Ireland,* in Letters Patents during her Coverture ; and of her Pedigree, conveying her three ways to the Crown ; First as descending from the Eldest Daughter of King *Henry VII,* another from the Duke of *Somerset,* the third from a daughter of *Edmund* before the Conquest."

To modern readers it may seem that too much attention was paid to Mary's arms, but it goes to show the importance attached to heraldry in past centuries, and its significance as a factor in some historical events ; moreover, the dangerous position in which Elizabeth found herself must not be overlooked. Her title to the throne depended on the legality of Henry VIII's divorce of Catherine of Aragon. Supposing that divorce not to have been valid, as good Catholics maintained, Elizabeth was illegitimate, and Mary was the true Queen of England. In view of the Pope's proclamation releasing Elizabeth's subjects from their allegiance, and the presence of Catholic intriguers, Elizabeth had of necessity to keep a careful watch on Mary's designs, which were clearly reflected in her heraldry.

In her vicissitudes, Mary had the inspiration of a political cartoonist. Her industrious needle produced many devices, such as an ensnared lion overrun by hares, with the words, " Even the hares trample on the conquered lion " ; and camomile, with the legend, " Trampled upon, she giveth out greater fragrance." On the death of the Dauphin she adopted the device of sweet-rooted liquorice, with the motto, " The earth covers my sweetness."

A device which puzzled the English spies was a phœnix with the motto, *En ma fin ma commencement.* " It is a riddle that I understand not," wrote Nicholas Whyte to Cecil. One of Elizabeth's badges being a phœnix, could it not have meant that the phœnix Mary would arise from the ashes of the phœnix Elizabeth?

An emblem which was far clearer was a representation of two women on a wheel of Fortune, one of them, evidently Elizabeth, holding a lance, symbolic of war, and the other (Mary) a cornucopia for peace. Mary was obviously hoping for a turn of the wheel.

FIG. 180.—COLUMBUS.

FIG. 181.—THE DEVONSHIRE
DRAKES.

FIG. 182.—SIR FRANCIS DRAKE:
*Arms granted by Elizabeth to commemo-
rate his voyage round the World.*

There is hopelessness in another device consisting of a caged bird (Mary) with a hawk (Elizabeth) hovering over it, and the motto, " It is ill with me now, and I fear worse betides me."   Another represented the sun (Mary) eclipsed by the moon (Elizabeth), with the stinging words, " She taketh the light she envies."

Mary's pride and hope in her son was expressed by a lioness with a cub beside her : " One only, but a lion."

Sir Francis Drake.

The break with Rome gave England the excuse for challenging the Spanish and Portuguese monopoly in the newly-found western lands which had been divided between the Iberian countries by Pope Alexander VI.

Continental heraldry gives us a note on the early progress of geographical expansion.   The pictorial arms of Christopher Columbus are expressive of his discovery of a new world.   The first and second quarters contain a gold castle on red and a red lion on silver (for Castile and Leon), indicating royal favour.   The third refers directly to the lands he found, showing a stretch of blue ocean dotted with islands and bordered by a line of silver sand, both islands and shore bearing tropical trees and golden grain.   Between the third and fourth quarters is a space containing wavy white and blue bars, representing the sea ; and in the fourth are five gold anchors on blue (Fig. 180). A rhyming motto neatly explains the arms :

> " *A Castilla y a Leon*
> *Mundo nuevo dio Colon.*"

" To Castile and Leon Columbus gives a new world."

The discoveries of Columbus necessitated a change in the heraldry of the King of Spain.   The supporters of the Spanish arms were two columns, representing " the pillars of Hercules " (Gibraltar and Ceuta), which the ancients had regarded as the bounds of the habitable world.   The Spanish motto, *Ne Plus Ultra*, referred to these supporters.   Charles V now removed the negative word, thus affirming that there was more beyond the gates of the Mediterranean, and the words *Plus Ultra* still stand in the shield of Gibraltar (Fig. 218).

Into the jealously preserved seas of Spain burst Francis Drake, who, in 1577, with Elizabeth's connivance, sailed westward to harry the Spanish shipping. After seizing a large treasure, he continued his westerly voyage, and reached England after circumnavigating the globe.

This feat earned him a knighthood, and he assumed as his arms the red wyvern, or " fire drake," of the Devonshire Drakes (Fig. 181), with whom, however, he could not prove kinship. But he found that piracy, though encouraged against the Spaniards on the high seas, was not to be tolerated in armorial matters at home. Sir Bernard Drake, the lawful owner of the wyvern, distinguished himself by boxing Frankie's ears, apparently with impunity, demanding, " by what right he had assumed his family arms ? He (Sir Bernard) was the only Drake who had the right to bear the wyvern."

Frankie was literally crestfallen, till Elizabeth told him " that he had earned better arms for himself, which he should bear by her special favour." She thereupon gave him the arms and crest which commemorate his famous voyage (Fig. 182).

The shield is black, and bears a silver wavy fess (denoting the course of his voyage) between two Pole stars. The crest is a ship under ruff, being drawn round a globe by the hand of God, which issues from clouds. The motto above the crest is, *Auxilio Divino*, and another beneath the shield runs, *Sic parvis magna*. In the stern of the ship is a red dragon (*draco*), alluding to the name.

The next time he met Sir Bernard, Sir Francis asked him what he thought of the arms the Queen had given him.

" The Queen may have given you finer arms than mine," returned Sir Bernard, "but she cannot give you the right to bear the wyvern, the cognisance of my house."

Agnes Strickland, who tells this story, says that Drake added to his ship-crest Sir Bernard's red wyvern, hung up to the rigging by its heels. He did not altogether abandon his claim to the wyvern, for some representations of his arms show the monster quartered with the coat specially granted by Elizabeth, as though to imply that in spite of Sir Bernard, Francis regarded himself as a member of the armorial Drakes.

On Drake's arms the scholars of Winchester College made this verse, and nailed it to the mast of his ship :

" Plus ultra Herculeis, inscribas, Drace, Columnis,
    Et magno, dicas, Hercule, major ero.
Drace, pererrati quem novit terminus orbis,
    Quemque simul mundi vidit uterque Polus ;
Si taceant homines, facient te sidera notum.
    Sol nescit comitis non memor esse sui."

" Drake, *Plus Ultra* you write on the Pillars of Hercules ; and, ' great though Hercules,' you say, ' I will be greater.' " But for the omission of these lines, the verse is well rendered in the following translation of Elizabethan date :

" Sir Drake, whom well the world's ends knew
    Which thou didst compass round,
And whom both poles of heaven once saw
    Which North and South do bound,
The stars above would make thee known
    If men were silent here.
The sun himself cannot forget
    His fellow traveller."

" Sidera," of course, refers not so much to " the stars above " as to the stars in Drake's shield, and " the very stars " might have been a better translation.

Arms identical in design with Drake's, but different in colour, were assumed by Admiral van Noort, who first led the Dutch fleet through the Straits of Magellan some years after Drake's famous voyage. This is a regrettable piece of plagiarism.

We find no heraldic reference to the Armada, but some medals struck to commemorate its defeat are of interest. One shows a bay tree on an island, immune from lightning which bursts from surrounding clouds. Another shows the Ark floating "calmly on a raging sea," referring to the English flagship, the *Royal Ark*. Another bears the inscription, *Venit, vidit, fugit*, " It came, it saw, it fled "—a parody of Cæsar's motto.

Another medal depicts the Pope sitting in conclave with kings, apparently unaware of spikes which spring up from the floor. On the reverse is the Armada in flight.

" The guilt of the slave trade rests with John Hawkins, whose arms—a demi-Moor proper bound with a cord—commemorate his priority in the transfer of negroes from Africa to the labour fields of the New World " (J. H. Green, *Short History*).

Dudley.

The military assistance which Elizabeth rendered to the Netherlands in 1586 has record in the devices of Robert Dudley, Earl of Leicester, who was in charge of the expedition. Dudley's arms were a green double-tailed lion on gold, but in the Netherlands he set this aside in favour of the bear and ragged staff which he derived from his father, who as Earl of Warwick used these ancient Warwick badges. Dudley's incompetence as a general provoked a wit to write under his bear : *Ursa caret cauda non queat esse leo* :

> " As the bear lacks a tail,
> For a lion he'll fail."

When Leicester relinquished his command he sought to throw the blame for his failure on those whom he had gone to aid, by issuing a

medal representing sheep deserted by their dog, who as he trots off castigates them in dog-Latin as " not a flock but thankless beasts."

Dudley's fondness for symbolical devices showed itself in some of his gifts to Elizabeth, daringly indicating his affectionate aspirations. In 1574 he gave her a jewelled fan decorated with his white bear lying at the feet of a royal lion. He went still further when he presented her with a headdress adorned with his ragged staff intertwined with true-lovers' knots.

FIG. 183.—DUDLEY.

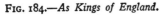

FIG. 184.—*As Kings of England.*   FIG. 185.—*As Kings of Scotland.*

ROYAL ARMS OF THE STUARTS

XVII

GREAT BRITAIN

" The Lion and the Unicorn
Were fighting for the Crown."

THREE years before her death Elizabeth showed positive recognition of James VI of Scotland as her successor, when she remarked that " the King of Scotland would become one day King of Great Britain." " The fact is deeply interesting, that it was from the lips of this last and mightiest of England's monarchs, that the style and title by which her royal kinsman and his descendants should reign over the united kingdoms of the Britannic Empire was first pronounced. It surely ought not to be forgotten that it was Queen Elizabeth herself who gave that prospective empire the name of Great Britain " (Agnes Strickland).

But James could not, in fact, call himself King of Great Britain because there was no real fusion of the realms. His accession medal styled him, " Emperor of the British Isle and King of France and Ireland "; another, " Cæsar Augustus of Britain and heir to the Cæsars." Parliament in its first address hailed him, " of the realms and kingdoms

171

of England, Scotland, France and Ireland, the most potent and mighty King." Not until Anne's reign, when complete union was achieved, did the phrase " Great Britain " occur in the official royal style, but the proclamation of 1606 creating the Union Jack referred to " this Isle and Kingdom of Great Britaine," so the conception which Elizabeth first expressed was not allowed to lapse.

Henricus Rosas Regna Jacobus—" Henry (united) the roses, James the kingdoms "—was a favourite motto of James I, drawing a parallel between his position and that of the first Tudor king, and cunningly reminding his English subjects that although a Scotsman by birth he was descended from Henry VII. It was suggested by Parliament's first address to him, which opened thus :

> " Great and manifold were the benefits, most dread and most gracious Sovereign, wherewith Almighty God blessed this kingdom and nation by the happy union and conjunction of the two noble houses of York and Lancaster, thereby preserving this noble realm, formerly torn and almost wasted with long and miserable dissension and bloody civil war ; but more inestimable and unspeakable blessings are thereby poured upon us, because there is derived and grown out of that union of those two princely families, a more famous and greater union, or rather a re-uniting, of two mighty, famous and ancient kingdoms (yet anciently but one) of England and Scotland, under one Imperial crown, in your most royal person."

The Arms of Great Britain.

As Henry VII had expressed the union of York and Lancaster by the Tudor rose, so James symbolised the " greater union " which his accession effected, by combining the arms, supporters and badges of his two realms.

But the new Royal Arms were not produced without contention. From their first introduction to one another, the lion and the unicorn began to squabble for precedence, clearly showing that the two nations were as yet unprepared for anything more than a nominal union.

The revision of the Royal Arms was made the occasion for including the Irish harp (hitherto borne separately, and only for Irish purposes), and this was relegated without question to the third quarter of the shield. The question then arose whether the combined arms of France and England or the arms of Scotland should occupy the first quarter.

To Englishmen to-day the point may seem trivial. Asked for a decision, we should say that the Sovereign normally lives in England; that Parliament meets here; that England contains most of the great centres of business and industry; that she is the senior and more populous kingdom; and that clearly her arms should take the first place.

But look at the matter from the point of view of the Scottish people in the early seventeenth century. Their King had acquired the throne of England by inheritance. He was King of Scotland before he was King of England. England might be the wealthier and more populous realm, and King James might find it convenient to spend most of his time there. But this did not alter the fact that it was Scotland that had added to her dominions by the acquisition of England, and not the other way round. The Scottish arms, therefore, should take premier place in the shield.

It was sound reasoning. The ordinary law of heraldry assigns the first quarter of a shield to a man's paternal arms, and the subsequent quarterings (as many as may be necessary) to the arms of other families which he may represent by the marriage of his male ancestors with sundry heiresses. James's paternal arms were those of Scotland. His ancestor had married the daughter of Henry VII of England, and on Elizabeth's death James became heir to the royal Tudors, and was entitled to add their arms to his own in the second quarter of his shield.

On the other hand, the English heralds may reasonably have argued that in marshalling royal heraldry, which is official rather than personal, strict rules must give place to national considerations.

Ultimately a compromise was reached by varying the arms in the two countries. The arms of James I of England consisted of France and England quarterly in the first and fourth quarters, Scotland in the second and Ireland in the third (Fig. 184). But James VI of Scotland satisfied his northern subjects by placing the arms of Scotland in the first and fourth quarters, and those of England and France in the second (Fig. 185).

This variation in the Royal Arms north and south of the Tweed is still observed, a reminder that the English and the Scots remain distinct nations with distinct traditions and sentiments.

Under James I and VI, one of the unicorn supporters of the Scottish shield was adopted into the English arms in place of the Welsh dragon, which had been a supporter of the Tudors. In England the lion continued to hold the " dexter " place, and the unicorn took the " sinister." In Scotland they changed places.

The hostility which existed between the English lion and the Scottish unicorn before the two realms came under one crown is referred to by Spenser in *The Faerie Queene :*

> " Like as a Lyon, whose imperiall powre
> A prowd rebellious Unicorn defyes. . . ."

The origin of the unicorn as a Scottish emblem is uncertain, but we may recall that in the Middle Ages a religious significance attached to it. Inasmuch as it was fabled to lose its fierceness in the presence of a virgin, and to lie quiet at her feet, it was taken to be an emblem of Christ; while its single horn was supposed to be a symbol of the unity of the Father and the Son.

The First Union Jack.

A similar dispute to that which attended the union of the arms of England and Scotland arose in 1606 on the design of the first union flag—called the Union Jack, though strictly this term applies only when the flag flies from a jackstaff in a ship's bows.

The combination of the crosses of St. George and St. Andrew seemed a fitting way of symbolising the union of England and Scotland, and neither country objected to the principle, especially as it would overcome the difficulty presented by two flags: which should hold the highest place when they were flown from one mast. But both

countries found cause for complaint in the design of the new flag
(Fig. 186).

Scotland objected to the fact that the cross of St. George overlay
that of St. Andrew. " The flag will give occasion of reproach to this
nation," because " the Scots' cross, called St. Andrew's cross, is
twice divided, and the English cross, called St. George, drawn through
the Scots' cross, which is thereby obscured, and no token or mark to
be seen of the Scots' arms. This will breed some hate and miscon-
tentment betwixt your Majesty's subjects."

On the other hand, the English complained of the almost complete
disappearance of the white ground of St. George's cross.

However, no more satisfactory way of combining the flags could
be found, and the design was not amended.

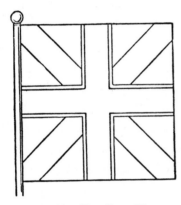

FIG. 186.—THE FIRST UNION
JACK.

FIG. 187.—THE UNION OF
ROSE AND THISTLE.

The Rose and Thistle.

Following his plan of uniting the national emblems, James combined the English rose with the Scottish thistle. He bore them sometimes springing from the same stalk, and sometimes dimidiated, that
is, half a rose joined with half a thistle (Fig. 187).

The origin of the thistle as the flower of Scotland is uncertain,
but legend says it commemorates a victory over the Danish raiders.
It is related that in 1010, in the reign of Malcolm I, an army of Danes

FIG. 188.—RAMSAY :
The Gowrie Conspiracy.

FIG. 189.—THE GUNPOWDER
PLOT MEDAL.

landed on the coast intent on attacking Stains Castle. They approached the place under cover of night, shoeless so as to make no noise. Reaching the moat they jumped in to swim it. But the moat contained a more sure defence than water ; it was dry and overgrown with thistles. The piercing yells of the bare-footed Danes roused the garrison, and just as the geese of the Capitol were venerated for having saved Rome, the thistle was thereafter held in esteem for having saved Scotland.

Unfortunately for a picturesque story the thistle did not make its appearance as a royal emblem in Scotland until the fifteenth century.

Plots against James's Life.

Shortly before his accession to the English throne, James had to deal with a conspiracy which, had it succeeded, would have changed the course of history. Despite the mystery which surrounds the Gowrie plot, it seems clear that in 1600 John Ruthven, Earl of Gowrie, made an attack on the King, and was slain in the act by John Ramsay. As a reward James added to the arms of Ramsay—a black eagle on gold—a coat of augmentation of blue, with a hand holding an upright sword piercing a heart and supporting a crown on its point (Fig. 188). The accompanying motto is, *Hæc dextra vindex principis et patriæ*— " This right hand is the safeguard of King and country."

Sir Thomas Erskine, later Earl of Kellie, on the same occasion won arms consisting of a crown within the Scottish tressure, both of gold on red.

That Gowrie actually meditated the seizure of the crown is suggested by a badge he was using about the time he came of age—an armed man stretching out his hand to grasp a crown.

The more famous conspiracy against James, the Gunpowder Plot, is not illustrated in heraldry, but a medal struck to commemorate it is of interest. It shows on one side a snake, representing the Jesuits, among the royal roses and lilies (Fig. 189), and on the other the name Jehovah, with the inscription, *non DorMItastI antIstes IaCobI.* The capital letters give the date of the plot, MDCIIIII.

Ireland and the Baronets.

Of the harp of Ireland, the Earl of Northampton wittily remarked, " The best reason that I can observe for the bearing thereof is that it resembles that country in being such an instrument that it requires more cost to keep it in tune than it is worth." Modern statesmen have put the same thought more diplomatically if less neatly.

The Irish question of James I's reign, and the steps he took to solve it, are commemorated in the arms of English baronets by the red hand of Ulster on a white escutcheon.

Following the rising of Hugh O'Neill, who might call himself Earl of Tyrone but aspired to be King of Ulster, James instituted the degree of baronets, " an hereditary dignity meane in place between the degree of a Baron and the degree of a Knight."

A condition imposed on each recipient of the honour was that " he shall bee Content to pay 30 foote after 8d. per diem for 3 yeares, towards the servyce of Ireland, and particularlie in regard to the plantacion of Ulster." But the degree was not merely for such as could purchase admission. It was stipulated that none should be made a baronet but those whose paternal grandfathers bore heraldic arms. In allusion to the special need which was met by the funds thus raised—about a thousand pounds from each baronet—the badge

N

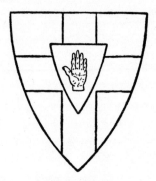

FIG. 190.—O'NEILL.   FIG. 191.—ULSTER.

of Ulster on a white shield was granted to every baronet to be placed in his arms as an indication of his rank.

The badge of the red hand was derived from the arms of the O'Neills, and is the subject of a romantic tale.   The ancestor of the O'Neills, it is said, was one of a party of Scandinavian adventurers who sighted the Irish coast.   Their leader promised the territory in view to the man who should first touch land.   There was a race for the shore, and as his boat neared it, the first of the O'Neills chopped off his left hand and cast it to the land.

Like so many other such stories it was probably invented to account for the arms of the O'Neills—a red hand, and in the lower part of the shield a salmon in water (Fig. 190).

The red hand became the emblem of Ulster when the O'Neills became its kings, and to-day denotes the members of the order which snatched away the land which once it grasped.

The modern arms of Ulster (Fig. 191) combine the red cross on gold of the De Burghs, Norman Earls of Ulster, with the O'Neills' red hand.

James's policy of colonisation in Ireland, which succeeded the restoration of comparative order, is recalled by the arms of Derry, which consist of " the picture of death (or a skeleton) sitting on a mossie stone, and in the dexter point a castle; and forasmuch as that cittie was since most trayterouslie sacked and destroyed by Sr. Carliere (or Sr. Charles) O'Dogharty and hath since been (as it were) raysed from the dead by the worthy undertayking of the Hoble. Cittie of London, in memorie whereof it is from henceforth called and known by the name of London Derrie." In the upper part of the shield are the arms of London, commemorating the London Trading Companies' help (Fig. 192). Coleraine (co. Antrim) also acknowledges London's aid by bearing her arms with the addition of a fish (perhaps the O'Neill salmon) in the second quarter (Fig. 193).

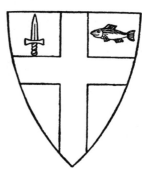

FIG. 192.—LONDONDERRY.   FIG. 193.—COLERAINE.

London Arms in Irish Towns.

FIG. 194.—COIN OF CHARLES I.

XVIII

THE ROYAL REPUBLIC

"The trappings of a monarchy would set up an ordinary commonwealth."—
Johnson, *Lives of the Poets*.

THE heraldry of Charles I's reign is silent as to the constitutional
struggle which came to a violent climax in 1642, and we must take
up the narrative at the point when Charles raised the royal banner at
Nottingham.

Inscribed on the King's banners was this declaration of policy:
"I will defend the laws of England, the liberties of Parliament, and
the Protestant religion." This appeared on some of his coins in the
contracted form: RELIG. PROT. LEG. ANG. LIBER. PAR.
together with the text, *Exurgat Deus Dissipentur Inimici*, "Let God
arise and let His enemies be scattered."

Some of the Royalist banners were in the nature of political
cartoons. One showed five hands reaching at a crown, defended by a
sixth, and bore the motto, *Reddite Cæsari*, as though to claim the
support of Christ's words for the Stuart doctrine of the Divine Right
of Kings.

180

Another banner displayed an ermine, with the motto, *Malo mori quam fœdari,* " I choose rather to die than to be sullied," an allusion to the idea that the ermine, symbol of royalty, will not survive the pollution of its fur.

The Parliamentary counterblow to the Royalist motto for the war was, *Pro Religione, Grege, et Rege,* which condensed their declared aims, " the safety of the King's person, the defence of both Houses of Parliament, and of those who have obeyed their orders and commands, and the preservation of true Religion, Laws, Liberties and Peace of the Kingdom."

The Scottish forces bore blue banners, inscribed in gold, " For Christ's Crown and Covenant." This colour may have been suggested by the field of St. Andrew's flag; and in choosing it the Covenanters also had in mind the injunction, in Numbers xv. 38, to the children of Israel to put upon the fringes of the borders of their garments " a ribband of blue."

Edgehill, Hereford and Newark.

Since arms are the tokens of honour, of which the King is the fount, it is to be expected that heraldic references to the Civil War deal entirely with the Royalist side of the struggle. Charles I and his son, for lack of more substantial means of rewarding gallant services, were lavish of heraldic honours.

Edgehill, the first battle, won Edward Lake a significant coat-of-arms. According to the grant, " he received sixteen wounds to the extreme hazard of his life, and his left arm being then disabled by a shot, he held his bridle in his teeth." The shield is red, and contains an armed hand holding a sword, from which floats a silver banner charged with a red cross and sixteen red shields representing his wounds, and on the cross is a lion of England (Fig. 195). The crest represents Lake himself on horseback, blood-spattered and in a fighting posture, holding his bridle between his teeth. He was later created a baronet.

Of the cities which remained loyal to the King, Hereford was singled out for armorial honours, " for there hath not any city since

FIG. 195.—LAKE :
Battle of Edgehill.

FIG. 196.—HEREFORD :
The Siege by Scottish troops.

this unnatural rebellion expressed greater fidelity and courage than the City of Hereford, in continuing their allegiance and resisting the many attempts of the rebels. But the greatness of their loyalty, courage and undaunted resolution did then most eminently appear when, being straitly besieged for a space of five weeks by a powerful army of rebellious Scots, and having no hopes of relief, they, joining with garrison and doing the duty of soldiers, then defended themselves . . . with so great destruction of the besiegers that they became the wonder of their neighbouring garrisons . . . and therefore do justly deserve such characters of honour " (Grant of Arms, 1645).

To the old arms of the city, three silver lions on red (perhaps derived from the Royal Arms), was now added a blue border charged with ten St. Andrew's crosses, clearly representing the besieging Scots (Fig. 196). The crest is a lion holding a sword ; and the supporters, two lions, each wearing a blue collar with three gold buckles, from the arms of Leslie, Earl of Leven, the Scottish General.

Another civic memorial of the war is the motto of Newark, " Trust God and sally," said to have been the exhortation of the Mayor to Lord Bellasyse during the siege of 1646.

A red rose on a gold canton was granted as an honourable addition to the arms of Captain Aylett, one of the most energetic Royalist soldiers, who is specially remembered for his heroic defence of Colchester.

The Loyal MacGregors.

The arms of the MacGregors, though of older date than the Civil War, provide a reminiscence of their refusal to join the Solemn League and Covenant. They consist of a silver shield containing a sword with an antique red crown on its point, crossing an oak tree (Fig. 197). The crown tells of their descent from King Alpin. It may also be taken as an emblem of their unwavering loyalty to the throne, which they maintained in spite of commissions of " fire and sword " against them, and the proscription of their very name—the just penalty for their marauding habits.

In refusing to join the Covenant against their King, the Mac-Gregors vowed " that as (in their arms) they bore the crown on the point of their sword, they would use the latter in defence of the former."

They threw in their lot with the ill-fated Montrose and assisted him in the rout of their enemies, the Campbells. For their loyalty to the House of Stuart they regained their name at the Restoration, and forfeited it again in William III's reign. Not until 1775 was the proscription of the name MacGregor finally repealed.

The oak tree in the MacGregor shield is the subject of a typical heraldic fable invented to account for particular arms. It is told that a twelfth-century MacGregor was instrumental in saving his King from a wild boar. As the beast was about to charge, MacGregor, with a nice but ill-timed regard for etiquette, asked the King's per-

FIG. 197.—MACGREGOR.

FIG. 198.—ROYALIST MEDAL.

FIG. 199.—RESTORATION MEDAL :
the Crown in the Oak Tree.

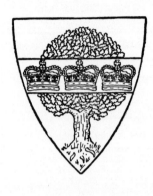

FIG. 200.—CARLOS :
Charles's companion in the Oak Tree.

FIG. 201.—NEWMAN :
Charles's flight from Worcester.

FIG. 202.—WHITGREAVE.

FIG. 203.—KEITH :
*Preservation of the Scottish
Regalia.*

THE WANDERINGS OF PRINCE CHARLES.

mission to defend him. "E'en do and spair nocht!" exclaimed the monarch hastily, whereupon MacGregor plucked an oak sapling out of the ground and slew the beast with it. Thus the oak tree came into the shield, while the King's words became the MacGregor motto.

A curious commentary on the events of 1648, when the Royalists made their last effort, is provided by a medal showing a diamond, symbolic of the King, splitting the hammer with which it is struck (Fig. 198). The hopes which this device reflected were shattered by the Parliamentary victories, followed by the death of Charles.

The design of the medal was perhaps suggested by a passage in Pliny :

> "Strike as hard as you will with an hammer upon the point of a Diamant, you shall see how it scorneth all blowes, and rather than it will seem to relent, first flieth the hammer that smiteth in peeces, and the very anvil itself underneath cleaveth in twaine."

The Flight of Prince Charles.

A series of arms granted " when the King enjoyed his own again " to those who had aided him, records the romantic adventures of Prince Charles after his father's death.

A red escutcheon bearing a crowned portcullis of gold added to the arms of Newman—black and white quarters with silver stars— acknowledges Colonel Newman's signal service in enabling Charles's escape through the gates of Worcester after the battle there (Fig. 201).

The famous oak,

> " Wherein the younger Charles abode
> Till all the paths were dim,
> While underneath the Roundhead rode
> And humm'd a surly hymn,"

is found in the arms of Colonel Careless, who shared the Prince's leafy shelter and attended him in his subsequent wanderings. Careless, whose unfitting name Charles changed to the regal-sounding one of Carlos, bore the oak on a gold shield, and across it a red fesse charged with three royal crowns (Fig. 200). The crest was a crossed sword and sceptre within a wreath of oak

Arms of identical design with Carlos's, but with a silver field and black fesse, were used by the family of Penderel of Boscobel, on whose land the oak stood, as a token of their having given the Prince shelter, hospitality and clothing.

These arms should be compared with the design on the reverse of Charles II's coronation medal showing the oak tree bearing three crowns (standing either for the three Stuart kings or the three kingdoms) and surrounded by the motto, *Iam florescit* (Fig. 199).

Francis Wolfe, who for a short time sheltered Charles at his house at Madeley, was granted the royal crown to be upheld by the wolf he bore as a crest.

From Boscobel the Prince went to Moseley, where he hid in the house of one Whitgreave, whose staunchness in denying Charles's presence, even under threats, earned a grant to his descendants of a red rose within an oak wreath, to be placed on a silver chief in their shield containing a gold cross "quarter-pierced" on blue, with four red chevrons on the cross (Fig. 202).

These arms show the introduction of a new emblem into our national insignia, the oak wreath, which Charles adopted after his adventure in the oak; it has become as characteristic an English emblem as the rose; witness its appearance on our sixpences and threepenny-pieces, and the battleship named *Royal Oak*.

Of this group of heraldic honours, the most remarkable is that granted to the family of Lane for the assistance given to Charles by Mistress Jane Lane, for many years after a Royalist toast. Mistress Jane aided the Prince's escape from his foes by agreeing that he should pose as her servant, in which guise he rode before her on a strawberry roan horse to Bristol, where he hoped to take ship for France.

Mistress Lane's courageous loyalty earned for her family one of the most notable augmentations known to heraldry, none other than the three lions of England. They were added as a canton to the Lane arms—a shield divided horizontally gold and blue, with a red chevron, and three stars counter-coloured. The accompanying crest is the faithful strawberry roan, holding a crown in token that he once carried its owner, and the motto is *Garde le Roy* (Fig. 204).

To Francis Mansell of Guildford, who found the ship in which Charles eventually sailed from Shoreham, was granted a lion of England as an addition to his arms, with the crest of a ship flying St. George's cross and with three crowns on the stern (Fig. 205).

The preservation of the regalia of Scotland by a member of the Keith family, who buried it in the church at Kinneff to save it from the Parliamentarians, is commemorated by an augmentation now borne by the Earl of Kintore (Fig. 203). This is a red shield with the Scottish crown, sceptre and State sword within a ring of golden thistles. The shield is placed on the old arms of Keith—silver, a gold chief with three red pallets. The accompanying motto is, *Quæ amissa salva*, "What was lost is safe." The crown, sword, and sceptre also appear in the modern arms of Kincardineshire, together with Dunnottar Castle, where the "honours of Scotland" were guarded before their removal to Kinneff.

FIG. 204.—LANE:
Charles's escape to Bristol.

FIG. 205.—MANSELL:
Charles's escape from England.

Commonwealth Heraldry.

The execution of Charles I, the declaration of the kingship to be " unnecessary, burdensome and dangerous to the liberty, safety and public interest of the people," and the proclamation of a commonwealth—these events produced an eclipse of the Royal Arms. In many places they were defaced or removed ; but even a commonwealth must have its heraldry, and it is a fact of some historical significance that the emblems of royalty were not completely abandoned.

The lions and fleurs-de-lys of Plantagenet, Tudor and Stuart were too closely connected with the hereditary monarchy to find any place in republican symbolism, and in their stead England and Scotland fell back on popular and impersonal insignia—the crosses of their

FIG. 206.   FIG. 207.

COMMONWEALTH COINS.

patron saints. Ireland retained her harp. Coins of the Commonwealth show on the reverse separate shields containing St. George's cross and the Irish harp surrounded by the motto, " God with us " (Fig. 206).

When Oliver Cromwell assumed the Protectorate, the tokens of England, Scotland and Ireland were once more grouped in one shield, and a personal character was given to the Commonwealth Arms by the inclusion of Cromwell's own shield (Fig. 207).

Cromwell was by paternal descent a member of a Welsh family named Williams. He derived his surname from his great-grandfather, Sir Richard Williams, alias Cromwell, who had taken the latter name from his mother, a sister of Henry VIII's famous minister. But while he changed his name, this Sir Richard retained the arms of Williams, a white lion rampant on black, which he transmitted to his descendants, including Oliver.

It is interesting to find that Cromwell's crest contained a mark of royal honour. It consisted of a half-lion holding a diamond ring. The lion formerly held a javelin, but in 1540 Sir Richard Williams distinguished himself in a tournament before Henry VIII, who presented him with a ring, bidding him add it to his crest.

The Republic's complete display of heraldry (Fig. 208) appeared on the reverse of the Great Seal of 1655. A blend of the emblems of the old realm and the new commonwealth which do not seem to harmonise with one another, these arms reflect the state of the country with remarkable truth. The heraldic supporters of the Tudors, last used by the royal and imperious Elizabeth, maintain an unregal shield in the centre of which are the arms of a man whom Elizabeth would secretly have admired, and publicly denounced as a traitor. Over this shield is set the six-barred helmet of monarchy, surmounted by the kingly crown and the lion-crest of the Plantagenets; and below it is the motto of the Republic, *Pax Quæritur Bello*, " If you seek peace, prepare for war," telling of the Protector's foreign policy : armed opposition to Spain as the foe of Protestantism and the monopolist of trade.

Cromwell and his officers must have given much thought to this composition, and it is worth while trying to detect their motives.

In the first place, the retention of certain royal emblems—crest, crown, helmet and supporters—suggests that Cromwell recognised that, whatever an extremist Parliament might decide, monarchy was too old and too revered a British institution to be permanently destroyed by the enactment of an unpopular assembly ; and that though the Republic could not display the old Royal Arms, it was politic to preserve the other insignia of royalty, both to satisfy popular sentiment and to provide against the time when the kingship might be revived. Cromwell himself refused the crown, but he preserved it for someone else's head.

Another suggestive feature of the seal is the substitution of the

FIG. 208.—ARMS OF THE COMMONWEALTH.

Welsh dragon for the Scottish unicorn as a supporter, due partly, perhaps, to the fact that Cromwell himself was of Welsh extraction, but more probably to a desire to avoid incorporating in the arms any reminder of the House of Stuart. Policy, perhaps delicacy, perhaps conscience, forbade Oliver to use this emblem of the royal family whose downfall he had produced, and in reverting to the dragon he harked back to the days of Elizabeth, as much as to suggest that the Stuarts had never been.

According to Sir Bernard Burke, when Oliver's coffin was opened a copper plate was found engraved with the arms of England impaling those of Cromwell.

Heraldry seems to show not only that Oliver recognised the transitory nature of the Republic, but that he regarded himself as holding the monarchy in trust—that throughout the Commonwealth and Protectorate, England remained a kingdom at heart.

The Stuarts Restored and Exiled.

Pepys tells us of the fall of the Commonwealth heraldry at the restoration of the King's. On May 11th, 1660, he wrote :

> " This morning we began to pull down all the State's arms in the fleet, having first sent to Dover for painters and others to come to set up the King's."

Two days later :

> " To the quarter deck, at which the taylors and painters were at work cutting out some pieces of yellow cloth in the fashion of a Crown and C.R., and put it upon a fine sheet, and that into the flag instead of the State's arms."

Charles II signalised his return by such grants of heraldic honours as have been described above, and too often an augmentation was inadequate compensation for lands lost and coffers depleted in the King's service.

He also thought of commemorating the Restoration by founding a new order of knighthood to be known as the Knights of the Oak, and to be distinguished by a silver badge depicting the King in the Oak. But the idea was abandoned for fear of stimulating animosities which were better forgotten.

It was at this time that oak leaves were introduced into the coronets of the Kings of Arms.

The Stuarts in exile are recalled in heraldry by a grant of arms made by " James III and VIII " to John Graeme, Earl of Alford, consisting of the Royal Arms of Scotland laid upon the saltire of St. Andrew, the colours being blue and white countercoloured, *i.e.* the lion and tressure are blue where they lie on the white saltire and white where they lie on the blue field.

The Jacobites took as their emblem the white rose which had been the emblem of legitimism in the Wars of the Roses, and this gave rise to the white cockade which they wore on their hats.

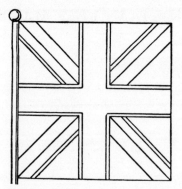

FIG. 209.—THE SECOND UNION JACK.

XIX

EMPIRE AND INDUSTRY

" If heraldry were guided by reason, a plough in a field arable would be the most noble and ancient of arms."—Cowper, *Of Agriculture.*

IT is unfortunate that heraldry should have reached its artistic nadir at the very moment when it was needed to record the series of naval and military exploits which attended the expansion of Britain. The wars of the eighteenth and nineteenth centuries left many arms the richer for an augmentation but the poorer in beauty, for many of these additions not only were ugly in themselves but overburdened a hitherto pleasing shield with a wealth of detail entirely foreign to the simple forms of antique heraldry. Neptunes and Britannias, war medals, fortifications and even complete battle pictures find their place in the crowded armorials of this period. They form a tedious and uninspiring record, and a few examples must suffice to indicate the tenor of them all. A glance through the pages of an illustrated peerage will provide anyone who may be interested with further instances.

The period of heraldic debasement corresponds roughly with the Hanoverian dynasty. The historical heraldry of the pseudo-Stuarts, with which we have first to deal, is quite in keeping with the older tradition.

Royal Heraldry from Stuart to Windsor.

The accession of William III to the throne of his uncle and father-in-law, James II, gave the heralds the task of amending the Royal Arms for the second time within the century.

The banner which the Prince of Orange bore on his entry into the realm displayed in addition to the British arms a number of foreign quarterings which, in deference to the insular prejudices of his new subjects, he soon dropped, retaining only his paternal shield of Nassau—gold billets and a lion rampant on blue. This he bore in the centre of his maternal shield, the Royal Arms of the Stuarts, which were repeated on the sinister side of the shield as the arms of Mary Stuart, his wife.

This arrangement of the Royal Arms indicated the position of William and Mary as joint sovereigns with equal rights, a status on which William had to insist against, on the one hand, those who wished him to be regarded as a mere regent in the absence of James II, and on the other those who desired Mary to be queen-regnant, with William as her consort. Had William been but regent or consort, the Royal Arms would have stood as they were in the reigns of the Stuart kings.

At Mary's death, William dropped her arms from the sinister side of the shield, and bore the Royal Arms with the Nassau inescutcheon (Fig. 210).

William's motto was, *Je Maintiendray,* referring to the words inscribed on the banner under which he landed in England, " The Protestant Religion and Liberties of England."

As a badge he used the orange of his continental principality. A medal commemorating his accession shows a flourishing orange tree standing beside the fallen oak of the Stuart dynasty.

Oranges were granted as heraldic tokens of honour to some of those who assisted William to the English throne. A crowned orange on a blue escutcheon was added to the arms of Sir Francis Hume—three silver engrailed piles on red—who was also rewarded with the barony of Polwarth, to which this coat-of-arms still appertains (Fig. 212). Three oranges within a golden tressure of thistles on blue were granted

o

FIG. 210.—WILLIAM III.   FIG. 211.—ANNE (*after* 1707).

to Livingstone, Viscount Teviot, to commemorate his part in the Glorious Revolution.

From William's title and badge were derived the name and distinctive colour of the " Orange " societies of Irish Protestants. The colour has been inherited, through the Whigs, by modern Liberals, and is still used as a party colour in some constituencies at election times.

Queen Anne, of course, dropped the Nassau shield from the Royal Arms, and for the first five years of her reign she bore the arms as they had been displayed by the Stuarts.

As if to point out that after a period of foreign occupation the throne was now filled by a native sovereign, she caused her coronation medal to bear a crowned heart, encircled by a wreath of oak and mistletoe, with the legend, " Entirely English," a reference to these words from her coronation address :

> " As I know my own heart to be entirely English, I can sincerely assure you there is not anything you can expect or desire from me which I shall not be ready to do for the happiness and prosperity of England."

As if to link her fortunes with those of the former queen-regnant, she adopted Elizabeth's motto, *Semper Eadem.*

In 1707 the Act for the Union of the Two Kingdoms of England and Scotland was passed, and amongst other things provided " that the Ensigns Armorial of the said United Kingdom be such as Her Majesty shall appoint, and the Crosses of St. George and St. Andrew be cojoined in such manner as Her Majesty shall think fit."

The constitutional change was aptly expressed by impaling (*i.e.* placing side by side) in the first and fourth quarters of the royal shield the arms of England and Scotland, with France in the second quarter and Ireland in the third (Fig. 211). Thus the arms of France, which had occupied the premier place since the reign of Edward III, were relegated to the secondary position justified by their merely antiquarian significance, and this proved to be a preliminary to their abandonment.

Great Britain now came into official existence, with the Union Jack of James I's reign (which had passed out of use during the Commonweath) as its flag. Anne also revived the badge of the rose and thistle growing from the same stalk.

On the accession of George I (grandson of Charles I's sister Elizabeth), place had to be found in the royal shield for the arms of the Electorate of Hanover, which were placed in the fourth quarter (Fig. 213). Far from being wholly foreign to English heraldry, the Hanoverian quarterings brought into our arms two features which were quite at home in this country. They consisted of (i) two gold lions on red, for Brunswick; (ii) red hearts and a blue lion rampant on gold, for Luneberg; (iii) a white horse on red, for Westphalia; and in the

FIG. 212.—POLWARTH, *a crowned orange co nmemorating the " Glorious Revolution " that gave the Prince of Orange the crown.*

FIG. 213.—GEORGE I,
GEORGE II, *and*
GEORGE III,
until 1801.

centre, Charlemagne's crown on a red inescutcheon, the symbol of an Elector of the Holy Roman Empire. The first and third of these quarterings were old friends.

The two lions of Brunswick were, as it were, the offspring of our King Henry II's lions, Henry's daughter having married an ancestor of the House of Brunswick-Luneberg, to whom she carried her father's emblems. They were therefore near cousins of the three lions of England, and George I's heraldry proclaimed him to be rather less of a foreigner by descent than by personal characteristics.

The horse of Westphalia was a collateral descendant of the Frisian horse, whence sprang the arms of Kent (Chapter III), and was thus the only emblem with Anglo-Saxon associations that has ever appeared in our Royal Arms, except for the coat of Edward the Confessor embodied by Richard II.

The royal shield continued in this form during the reigns of George II and George III, until, following the Irish rebellion of 1798, the United Kingdom of Great Britain and Ireland came into being, when a further revision became necessary.

Hitherto the status of Ireland as a separate kingdom outside the union which embraced England and Scotland had been indicated by the fact that the harp occupied a quarter of the shield to itself. Now

Ireland had to be placed on a similar footing to Scotland, whose arms occupied one quarter with England's. As art forbade that the arms of the three countries should, as it were, lie three in a bed, policy demanded that the Scottish lion should leave his place beside his English brethren and once more occupy a quarter to himself.

This was made possible by the removal from our arms of the French fleurs-de-lys; and probably owing to the extinction of the French kingship, which made George III's style as King of France more archaic than ever, the occasion was taken to abandon not only the arms but the title of France.

The Royal Arms were then rearranged as shown in Fig. 214, the shield of Hanover being topped by an electoral bonnet. In 1816, when Hanover became a kingdom, this was exchanged for a crown (Fig. 215), and the arms continued in this form until 1837.

Through the operation of the Salic Law, the crown of Hanover passed to the Duke of Cumberland at William IV's death, and the arms of Hanover were consequently removed from our royal shield. With the accession of Victoria, therefore, the Royal Arms took the form in which they stand to-day.

FIG. 214.—GEORGE III, 1801–1816.

FIG. 215.—GEORGE III, *after* 1816.
GEORGE IV and WILLIAM IV.

Only by the Sovereign are the Royal Arms borne alone and without any differencing mark.   The other members of the Royal Family bear them with a label—a narrow bar across the top of the shield with three or five pendants.   The Prince of Wales has a plain white label with three pendants, and places in the centre of the royal shield an escutcheon of the arms of Wales ensigned with his coronet, which is similar in design to the Royal Crown but has only one arch.

The abdication of King Edward VIII set the heralds a new problem of devising arms for a former Sovereign.   This was met by restoring the white label he bore as Prince of Wales, and charging it with the Royal Crown in token of his former sovereignty.

Princess Elizabeth, Duchess of Edinburgh (now Queen Elizabeth II), bore the Royal Arms with a white label with three pendants, the middle one charged with a Tudor rose and each of the others with the cross of St. George.   The label of Princess Margaret bears a thistle between two Tudor roses.

The Union Jack.

At the union with Ireland in 1801, the Union Jack reached its final form by the introduction of the red diagonal cross of St. Patrick, as the FitzGerald saltire had now become.   It was first placed dead in the centre of St. Andrew's cross, but this roused another protest from Scotland.   Never having been wholly reconciled to the fact that the cross of St. George overlay that of St. Andrew, the Scots were now angered that their emblem should be still further obscured, becoming, as it seemed, no more than a white background to St. Patrick's cross.

This objection was met by moving St. Patrick's cross well out of the centre of St. Andrew's, which accounts for the fact that to-day the white diagonal stripes are broader on one side of the red pieces than on the other.   The thinner line of white represents the background of St. Patrick's cross, while the broader is the cross of St. Andrew.   The latter, as the senior emblem, takes precedence, the flag being flown in such a way that near the staff the broad white stripe of St. Andrew's cross is above the red diagonal of St. Patrick's (Fig. 209).

Marlborough.

William III's accession and Louis XIV's espousal of the Stuart cause drew England into a league against France. An augmentation in the arms of the Churchill family commemorates the Duke of Marlborough's victories, leading to the Treaty of Utrecht.

John Churchill's paternal arms were a white lion rampant on black, with the addition of St. George's cross on a canton, which had been granted to his father, Sir Winston Churchill, Captain of Horse to Charles I.

His victories under Anne won him his dukedom together with a further heraldic honour, a silver escutcheon of St. George's arms surmounted by the shield of France. His descendants bear this augmentation on the quartered shield of Churchill and Spencer (Fig. 216). Thus it came about that Sir Winston Churchill very fittingly bears on his shield the cross of St. George and the arms of France.

Marlborough's exploits on land were seconded by the achievements of British seamen, which in heraldry are typified by the arms awarded to Sir Cloudesley Shovel in reference to his victory over a combined French and Turkish fleet—a red shield with a silver chevron, two

FIG. 216.—CHURCHILL.

FIG. 217.—SHOVEL.

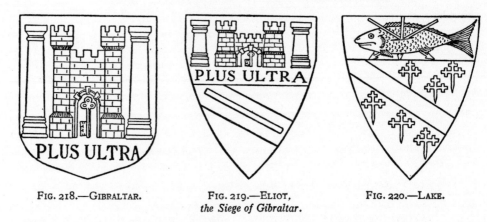

FIG. 218.—GIBRALTAR.

FIG. 219.—ELIOT,
the Siege of Gibraltar.

FIG. 220.—LAKE.

Turkish crescents and a fleur-de-lys of France (Fig. 217). These arms also remind us of the understanding between France and Turkey, which was a recurrent factor in European politics throughout the struggle between Bourbons and Hapsburgs.

Gibraltar.

The capture of Gibraltar in 1704 was the most important martial event of Anne's reign. The possession of the stronghold has ever since been a vital factor in British history, and its arms are noteworthy. They are of blue, with a castle standing between two columns, representing the Pillars of Hercules. In the doorway is a golden key, referring to Gibraltar's title, " the Key to the Mediterranean "; and beneath is the motto, *Plus Ultra* (Fig. 218).

These arms were added to the shield of Sir George Eliot, who also earned the barony of Heathfield by his defence of the Rock in the siege of 1779–83. The family arms were red with a gold bend and blue baton (Fig. 218). Another Eliot won a chief of honour in the form of the arms of Corsica—a Moor's head on white—marking his services as Viceroy of the island during the brief time that our George III was its King.

Eliot's Gibraltar augmentation was artistic as well as honourable. Other participants in the historic siege were less fortunate. Sir Roger

Curtis, for instance, was granted not the arms of the fortress but a representation of the Rock itself, " surrounded by fortifications and the sea."

Picture Postcard Heraldry.

This brings us to a brief review of those coats-of-arms which require a landscape painter rather than a heraldic artist for their proper display.

A sad example is the shield granted to Lord Harris, who was responsible for the defeat of Sultan Tippoo of Mysore. His arms were originally three hedgehogs (*heriz*), but by the time the heralds had completed their labours in Lord Harris's honour, the ancestral hedgehogs found themselves separated by a battlemented chevron bearing three hand grenades, and crushed down by a chief containing " a representation of the sally-ports of the capital and fortress of Seringapatam and drawbridge let down, and the Union Flag of Great Britain and Ireland hoisted over the standard of Tippoo Sultan." Tippoo's crowned tiger, pierced by an arrow and " charged on the forehead with the Persian character for ' Hydery,' " formed Harris's crest, while for supporters he was given a grenadier and a sepoy bearing respectively the Union Jack and the East India Company's flag, hoisted over Tippoo's banner and the French tricolour.

Contrast this with the Howards' dignified augmentation, or (to take an example contemporary with Harris) the heraldic honours given to Viscount Lake for service during the Mahratta War. To Lake's family arms—a silver bend and six crosslets on black—was added a silver chief with the fish of Mogul pierced by three spears (Fig. 220). This, being purely symbolical, is quite a pleasing piece of heraldry, and true to the best traditions of the craft.

Nelson and Trafalgar.

The most famous sufferer at the hands of the heralds was Lord Nelson. A black cross patonce on gold formed his original arms—a beautiful and simple shield which might have been dignified by some such augmentation as was granted to Marlborough. But the officers of arms, with an enthusiasm which far outran any artistic sense they might still possess, gave him first a red bend charged with another of gold, and thereon three exploding bombs. Then, to commemorate the Battle of the Nile, they loaded the shield with one of their pictorial chiefs, containing a disabled ship and a ruined battery, and between them (for local colour) a palm tree (Fig. 221). Two crests were placed above the shield, one consisting of the diamond plume of triumph presented to Nelson by Sultan Selim III as a reward for the Nile victory, and the other the stem of the Spanish man-of-war, *San Joseph.* A sailor holding a commodore's flag, and a British lion holding in its mouth the broken flags of France and Spain, supported the shield. Both supporters held a palm branch in reference to the motto, *Palmam qui meruit ferat.*

After Nelson's death at Trafalgar the arms were granted to his brother (created Earl Nelson), with the addition of the word TRAFAL-GAR across the shield. Similarly the name of the battle was added to the arms of Carnegie, Earl of Northesk, who was third in command (Fig. 222). The stem of a French man-of-war in flames was given him as a crest, while his two supporting leopards were decorated with representations of the medals struck to commemorate the victory. In the paw of each beast was placed a banner of St. George's cross, inscribed in gold, *Britannia Victrix.*

This illustrates the introduction of war medals into modern heraldry. They are unsatisfactory emblems when incorporated in a shield, because they are too small and "finicky" to be represented correctly in any but large reproductions of the arms.

The decline in the heralds' sense and appreciation of their own art at this time is further illustrated by the arms of Sir Isaac Heard, himself Garter King-at-Arms, who forsook his simple ancestral coat of silver with a red chevron and three black water bougets, for Neptune rising from the sea, holding a trident in his left hand and the top of a ship's mast in the other; and a blue chief with a Pole Star and two gold water bougets. This shield commemorated his preservation from drowning when washed overboard during a tornado off the coast of Guinea in 1750.

FIG. 221.—NELSON, *the Battle of the Nile.*   FIG. 222.—CARNEGIE : *Trafalgar.*

Wellington and Waterloo.

The arms of the Duke of Wellington indicate a return to the older and more artistic tradition in heraldic augmentation. The Duke bore the arms of Wellesley, a silver cross and twenty silver roundels on red, quartered with those of Colley, a red lion rampant with a coronet-collar on gold. In giving him armorial honours for the series of victories which culminated in Waterloo, the heralds wisely decided that no amount of elaboration would make so proud a token as the national crosses of the Union on an escutcheon (Fig. 223).

The Clark-Kennedys bear an augmentation commemorating the exploit of Sir Alexander Clark-Kennedy at Waterloo. He was in command of the centre squadron of the Royal Dragoons, and with his own hand captured the eagle and colours of the 105th Regiment. For this he was granted the captured colours, crossed by a sword, to be displayed on an ermine canton in his shield—silver, a red chevron and three black crosslets, with a red fleur-de-lys in the chief. The word WATERLOO is inscribed above the sword and colours.

The Union Jack supported by a golden lion on red appears in the arms of Lord Gough, who annexed the Punjab, but the composition is spoiled by the addition of the words CHINA : INDIA in the chief,

FIG. 223.—WELLINGTON.

FIG. 224.—KITCHENER.

and the fact that this coat-of-honour is quartered with one into which
are crowded Gough's ancestral boars' heads on blue, a red lion on a
silver fesse, the badge of the Spanish Order of Charles III, and in the
chief the fortress of Tarifa with a breach in the wall and the British
flag flying over the tower.

Kitchener of Khartoum.

More recent grants of arms to distinguished soldiers and sailors
have been innocent of such discordant devices as complete and realistic
fortresses and sea-fights. Lord Kitchener's shield, for instance, shows
a marked improvement on Lord Nelson's, though it is rather over-
crowded owing to the desire to make it as complete a record of his
military career as an entry in *Who's Who*. The field is red, and contains three bustards set about a blue chevron edged with silver; over
this is a golden pile with the British and Turkish flags circled by a
mural coronet inscribed KHARTOUM. The chief bears a lion of
England on red, between a black eagle and an orange tree, both on
silver (Fig. 224). There are two crests, an elephant's head holding a
sword (for his services in the East) and a stag's head, the neck pierced by
an arrow, and a golden horseshoe between the horns. A bridled
camel and a gnu are the supporters, and the motto is the single and
significant word, " Thorough."

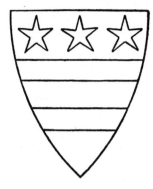

FIG. 225.—WASHINGTON.

FIG. 226.—ROSS-OF-
BLADENSBURG.

American Independence.

The idea that the " Star-spangled Banner " had its origin in the
arms of George Washington is well known, and possibly true. The
Washington shield, which dates at least from the reign of Richard II,
contains two red bars and three red stars on white (Fig. 225), whence,
it is said, the Stars and Stripes. But there is not much resemblance
between the Washington arms and the first of the American flags, that
of 1776, which had thirteen red and white stripes and in the canton
the old Union Jack. However, as Washington himself is said to
have suggested this design, it is possible that his own arms gave him
the idea of red and white stripes to represent the thirteen colonies.
When in the following year the united crosses of England and Scotland
were removed from the canton, thirteen stars in a ring on blue were
substituted, and again, the stars in Washington's shield *may* have
influenced the designers, though the committee of Congress stated
that the stars represented " a new constellation." On the whole, it
seems that the resemblance between the flag and Washington's shield,
though it may have influenced the designers, was not a primary consideration with them.

The ring of stars was abandoned in favour of rows of stars, and as
more states were added to the Union the number of stars and stripes
was correspondingly increased. But this was found to be inexpedient

FIG. 227.—THE UNITED STATES
OF AMERICA.

from the heraldic point of view, since it made the flag difficult to distinguish from a distance, and it was decided to maintain the number of
stripes at thirteen, representing the original states, and to vary the
number of stars, of which there are now fifty.

The United States shield differs from the flag. The stripes are
vertical, and instead of the canton there is a chief across the top of the
shield.   The chief is plain blue, but in some early instances of the arms
it was charged with stars. The shield is placed on the breast of an
eagle, one claw grasping an olive branch and the other thirteen arrows,
and above its head is a nimbus of thirteen stars with a scroll bearing the
motto, E PLURIBUS UNUM (Fig. 227).

The "Stars and Stripes" flag, drooping from a broken flag-
staff, appears in the shield of the family of Ross-of-Bladensburg,
to commemorate the achievements of Major General Robert Ross,
who, in 1814, beat the American troops at Bladensburg and burnt
Washington (Fig. 226).

Commonwealth Heraldry.

The development of the British Empire and Commonwealth has
enriched heraldry with beasts, birds and vegetation from distant parts
of the world, and emblems drawn from the mythology of other races.

The heraldry of the eastern lands provides examples of these innovations. An elephant in a grove of coco-nut palms formed the arms of Ceylon from 1906 until 1954 when it was replaced by a Sinhalese design of a lion grasping a sword on a circle bordered with lotus petals. Calcutta pays tribute to her natural scavengers by adopting two adjutant birds as supporters. Burma's peacock in a gold shield suggests the riches and splendour of the Orient, while Bombay's crest, a lion wearing an Eastern crown and holding a shield containing a sprig of the cotton tree, tells of the local cotton industry. The Indian tiger stands in the shield of Madras University, and above it is the sacred lotus flower and two white elephants' heads (Fig. 228). This tiger is a very different beast from the "tyger" of mediæval heraldry, which, being based on descriptions by travellers who do not seem to have had a very close view of the beast, consisted of a lion's body and tail, tufted mane, wolf's head and ears, with a single down-curving horn on the tip of its nose (Fig. 80). Tasmanian tigers are the supporters of the arms of Tasmania.

Canada.

As a fitting tribute to the French element in her history and population, Canada bears the fleurs-de-lys of France in a quartered shield together with the arms of England, Scotland and Ireland, and her own maple leaf badge in the base (Fig. 229). Quebec also places the fleurs-de-lys between the English lion and the maple leaf (Fig. 230).

In Canada's full display of heraldry the shield is supported by a lion and a unicorn, which differ from those in the Royal Arms of the United Kingdom in that the lion is uncrowned and holds a lance from which flies the Union Flag, while the unicorn has a lance with a flag bearing the fleurs-de-lys of France. The crest is a lion holding a maple leaf, and above it is placed the Royal Crown denoting Canada's status as a kingdom.

Manitoba bears a buffalo (Fig. 231), and Alberta and Saskatchewan indicate their wheat-fields (Figs. 232 and 233). British Columbia expresses its extreme westerly situation by wavy white and blue bars, representing the ocean, with a sinking sun (Fig. 234). Several of the States embody the cross of St. George or a lion of England. Nova

FIG. 228.—MADRAS UNIVERSITY.

FIG. 229.—CANADA.

FIG. 230.—QUEBEC.

FIG. 231.—MANITOBA.

FIG. 232.—ALBERTA.

FIG. 233.—SASKATCHEWAN.

FIG. 234.—BRITISH COLUMBIA.

FIG. 235.—NOVA SCOTIA.

FIG. 236.—GREENWICH.

FIG. 237.—AUSTRALIA.

FIG. 238.—NEW ZEALAND.

Scotia remembers Scotland in arms as in name, bearing three thistles on gold about a salmon on a blue wavy fesse (Fig. 235). This has replaced a much older shield showing St. Andrew's cross charged with the Scottish arms supported by a unicorn and a wild man.

A glimpse of Canadian development is provided by the arms of the late Lord Strathcona. A red shield contains a ramping half-lion, and in the base a canoe paddled by four men, with a flag bearing the letters N.W. for North-West Territory. On a silver fesse are a black hammer and nail, alluding to the fact that Strathcona drove the last nail on the completion of the Canadian Pacific Railway. The crest is the Canadian maple tree, with the Hudson's Bay Company beaver gnawing at its trunk.

Australasia.

The Southern Cross has a prominent place in the arms of both Australia and New Zealand (Figs. 237 and 238). The Australian shield also includes the English lion twice, the royal crown twice, a piping shrike and a black swan, each quarter standing for one of the states in the Commonwealth. In the New Zealand shield a wheat-sheaf, fleece and hammers denote her industries.

In these illustrations only the shields of Australia and New Zealand

P

are shown.   In the full heraldic display, Australia's shield is supported by a kangaroo and an emu standing against a background of golden wattle, and the crest is a seven-pointed star.   New Zealand's supporters are a female figure holding the Blue Ensign with the addition of four stars as in the first quarter of the shield, and a native in appropriate dress.   New Zealand formerly used the crest of a lion holding the Union Flag, but in 1956, with the Queen's approval, this was replaced by the Royal Crown.

Incidentally, the outstanding astronomical feature of the Northern Hemisphere, the Pole Star, appears in the arms of Greenwich, which, as the place where the world's time was formerly kept, displays an hour-glass.   These charges are placed on a blue pale between six blue stars on white (Fig. 236).

Africa.

While it was part of the Commonwealth of Nations, the Union of South Africa used arms assigned by Royal Warrant in 1910.   These consisted of a shield of four quarters containing emblems for the various states—a figure of Hope with her anchor for Cape Colony, two black wildebeesten for Natal, an orange tree for the Orange Free State, and a trek wagon in a green field for the Transvaal.   The shield was supported by a springbok and an oryx or gemsbok.

Antelopes are the supporters of Southern Rhodesia, and the crest is a representation of a strange bird carved in stone among the ruins of Great Zimbabwe.   Nyasaland's arms include the leopard of nature as distinct from the lion passant gardant sometimes termed "leopard" in ancient heraldry.

The arms of Tanganyika show an interesting development in heraldic art, an African native shield being used instead of the traditional shield-form of European chivalry.   The supporters, who stand on a representation of Mount Kilimanjaro, are a Tanganyikan man and woman each holding an elephant's tusk, the graceful curves of the tusks following those of the shield.   A cotton bush and a coffee bush grow at the feet of the supporters.   On the shield is a torch encircled by four interlacing rings (Fig. 239).

FIG. 239.—TANGANYIKA.

Industrial Heraldry.

Britain's transformation into an industrial country is reflected in the arms of many of the modern cities and towns which have resulted from the concentration of manufacturing populations.

The cotton industry is prominent in municipal heraldry in the north. Its emblems range from the sprigs of the cotton plant in the arms of Eccles and Darwen and the crests of Bury and Burnley, to shuttles and mules, hanks and bales of cotton in the arms of other Lancashire towns. Even the process of calico printing is depicted in the shield of Accrington.

Since the cotton industry owes so much to Sir Richard Arkwright, it is fitting to find a direct reference to his work in his arms, a cotton tree in a silver shield, and on a blue chief two gold roundels and a bee, emblem of industry.

Woollen manufactures are represented by such emblems as the fleece in the arms of Leeds (Fig. 240) and the ram and angora goat which support Bradford's shield.

Cotton, wool and coal-mining are all indicated in the arms of Morley, Yorkshire; the shield contains a sprig of cotton plant, two black pellets (representing lumps of coal) and a miner's pick and shovel, all on white, with a golden shuttle on a red fesse (Fig. 241). The crest is a shuttle and a ram's head.

FIG. 240.—LEEDS   FIG. 241.—MORLEY.   FIG. 242.—HARMSWORTH:
                                                        the Newspaper Industry.

The iron and steel and other metal industries are symbolised in civic arms by such things as hammers and anvils or (more emblematically) by the astronomical sign of Mars.   Metal workers are represented by Thor and Vulcan, who support the shield of Sheffield. A blast furnace forms the crest of Scunthorpe, but a number of towns in the Black Country prefer to represent furnaces in their arms by beacons or flaming towers, while Dudley does so by a salamander amid fire.

In the arms of Stoke-on-Trent the Potteries are indicated by the famous Portland vase in the British Museum, while the crest is a potter of Ancient Egypt.

The history of the railways is suggested by the arms of Darlington containing Stephenson's "Locomotion" and those of Swindon in which a more modern type of locomotive appears (Figs. 243 and 244). The objection is sometimes levelled against arms like those of Swindon that modern and ultilitarian objects are so far removed from the form and spirit of the mediæval art as to appear ridiculous in heraldry.   Yet in their day the sword and the spur, the portcullis and the water budget were modern and utilitarian objects, and if heraldry is to reflect the conditions and achievements of man in the twentieth century it must not reject emblems merely because they are new.   They will not be so for long.   The arms of Swindon were granted in 1901, and already the locomotive is a period piece, and in process of becoming an antiquity like that in the shield of Darlington.

Travel by air is represented by an aeroplane in the arms of Beddington and Wallington, and by a winged airscrew forming the crest of

FIG. 243.—DARLINGTON.   FIG. 244.—SWINDON.

THE GROWTH OF THE RAILWAYS

Hendon.   In the shield of Hayes and Harlington (Fig. 245) in addition
to a pair of wings there is a Y-shaped cross (a cross-pall) intended to
suggest the runways of London Airport as well as the pallium in the
arms of the See of Canterbury, with which Hayes was closely connected
for seven centuries.   The cog-wheels between lightning rays stand for
local electrical industries.   In the arms of Rugby and some other towns
an heraldic thunderbolt is used to represent
electrical works.

Paper-making is shown in the arms of
Sittingbourne by a roll of parchment, and in
those of Dartford by a jester's head in a "fool's
cap"—a device found as a watermark in paper
in the seventeenth century.

The newspaper press is represented by
crossed rolls of paper and bees in the arms of
the two peers named Harmsworth, the late
Lord Northcliffe, and Viscount Rothermere
(Fig. 242), whose supporters are gladiators.

FIG. 245.—HAYES AND
HARLINGTON.

FIG. 246.—THE ROYAL ARMS, *by Mr. Kruger Gray.*

XX

HERALDRY IN THE TWENTIETH CENTURY

THE present century has seen some interesting developments in the royal insignia, reflecting changes in the position of the monarchy with regard to Commonwealth countries, some of which are kingdoms while others have become republics.

The Great Seal of King George V made a striking departure from those of his predecessors, for while all our Kings from William the Conqueror to Edward VII (except Henry VI) were portrayed on the reverse of their seals on horseback, formerly in armour but latterly in robes and crown, King George V was depicted in naval uniform, standing on the deck of a battleship.

The obverse of the seal followed the traditional design of the monarch seated in state on the throne. Thus the pomp and ceremony of kingship were indicated on one side of the seal, while the other expressed the status of the British sovereign as chief and representative citizen of a Commonwealth of Nations linked by the seaways.

214

Following the establishment of the Irish Free State as a self-governing Dominion, the phrase "United Kingdom" was omitted from the royal title. George V was, "By the Grace of God, of Great Britain, Ireland, and the British Dominions beyond the Seas, King, Defender of the Faith, and Emperor of India."

When the Republic of Ireland was declared and left the Commonwealth, the United Kingdom became that of Great Britain and Northern Ireland. In 1948, when India and Pakistan became separate and independent states, the title "Emperor of India" was dropped. In the present reign, "Head of the Commonwealth" has been added to the royal style, and Her Majesty is "By the Grace of God, of the United Kingdom of Great Britain and Northern Ireland and of Her other Realms and Territories Queen, Head of the Commonwealth, Defender of the Faith."

Since Northern Ireland is still part of the United Kingdom the Irish harp has been retained in the Royal Arms. In essentials these have remained unchanged since 1837, though there have been variations in artistic treatment. Fig. 246 shows a design by Mr. Kruger Gray for the British Industries Fair, and Fig. 250 illustrates the arms as designed by Mr. Reynolds Stone and used on Stationery Office publications. The latter includes the form of heraldic crown approved by the Queen for use during her reign. Based on St Edward's crown, it differs from the one formerly used in that the arches are depressed at their intersection.

Scotland continues to display her distinctive Royal Arms, though they were at one time in danger of extinction owing to an extraordinary mistake made in the reign of George IV. When that monarch was due to make a state visit to Edinburgh, tabards for the Scottish officers of arms were ordered from a London tailor, who in all innocence supplied them according to the English design, with the English lions in the first and fourth quarters and the Scottish lion in the second. Unfortunately this mistake was taken as a precedent for dropping the Scottish style of the Royal Arms in other ways; but in recent years it has been restored, and in 1928 it was placed beyond all danger by the provision of a set of new tabards conforming to the Scottish tradition for the Lord Lyon King of Arms and the Scottish heralds.

FIG. 247.—THE QUEEN'S PERSONAL
FLAG.

FIG. 248.—BANNER OF THE DUKE
OF EDINBURGH.

The Queen and the Commonwealth.

The Royal Arms of the United Kingdom served as a symbol of sovereignty throughout the British Empire, since all the dominions and colonies owed allegiance to the Crown.   However there were those who felt that these arms, comprising only the coats of the three old kingdoms, did not reflect the position of the monarch in relation to the countries overseas, and it was suggested that there should be either a distinctive version of the Royal Arms for every dominion, or a composite imperial shield in which the several dominion arms would be quartered with those of the United Kingdom.

This became a matter of importance as the Empire developed into a Commonwealth of independent sovereign states, some of them kingdoms owing allegiance to the Queen, others republics acknowledging her not as their monarch but as Head of the Commonwealth. When Her Majesty visits these countries it would be inappropriate for her flag as Queen of the United Kingdom to be flown on aircraft, cars and buildings, whether in her other realms such as Canada and New Zealand, or in republican lands of which she is not the Queen.

Accordingly in 1960, prior to visits to India and Pakistan in the following year, Her Majesty adopted a personal flag, distinctive in design and not specifically associated with any one of the nations of

the Commonwealth.   This bears her initial E ensigned with the Royal
Crown and placed within a chaplet of roses, all gold on a blue ground
(Fig. 247).   The official description of the flag does not specify the
number of roses in the chaplet, which in fact may vary, but in the
original design there were eleven roses, which happened to correspond
with the number of sovereign states in the Commonwealth at the time
the flag was adopted.   New though it is, this flag has certain links with
royal heraldry of the past.   Its colours are those of Edward the Confessor's shield, and of the Garter (probably derived from the French
quarters in the old Royal Arms), while the golden roses recall the
badge used by Edward I (p. 69).

In this flag the Royal Crown is not intended to be a symbol of
governmental authority as it is in Great Britain.   It represents the
personal rank and dignity of queenship which Her Majesty retains
even when, as Head of the Commonwealth, she visits countries which
do not own her as their queen.

The Queen's personal flag does not supplant the "Royal Standard"
—the popular name for the banner bearing the Royal Arms.   This
remains Her Majesty's banner as Queen of the United Kingdom.

When planning her visit to Sierra Leone in 1961, the Queen herself
had the idea of a new personal flag to be used only in that country.
This consists of a flag of the arms of Sierra Leone charged in the centre
with the Queen's own device of the crowned E within the chaplet of
roses, all gold on a blue roundel (Fig. 249).   This became the first of
several personal flags for use when Her Majesty visits Commonwealth
countries of which she is Queen. Such flags were adopted for Canada
and New Zealand in 1962, each following the example of Sierra Leone
in having the Queen's device in the centre of a banner bearing the arms
of the country.   In the case of the flag for Australia, adopted in 1963,
the blue roundel enclosing the device is placed on a gold star of seven
points (such as forms the crest of Australia) in the middle of the six
quarterings of the arms shown in Fig. 237.

Other members of the Royal Family use flags bearing their arms
on suitable occasions.   Fig. 248 shows the banner of the Duke of
Edinburgh consisting of the quartered coats of Denmark, Greece,
Mountbatten and Edinburgh.

FIG. 249.—THE QUEEN'S PERSONAL
FLAG FOR SIERRA LEONE.

The World Wars.

The two World Wars produced an interesting revival of the utilitarian purpose of heraldry. The vast operations in the world-field of battle involved the use of immensely larger units than had ever before been known in warfare, and the old regimental badges were no longer adequate to identify troops. Badges were therefore devised for the various divisions and army corps, and were worn on the soldiers' sleeves and placed on transport, etc.

Some of these badges perpetuated old heraldic emblems, such as the red dragon of the 38th (Welsh) Division, the shamrock of the 16th (Irish), the thistle on St. Andrew's cross of the 52nd (Lowland), the red sword of St. Paul of the 56th (London), the red rose of the 55th (West Lancashire), the red and white roses of the 31st (York and Lancaster), and others.

The foregoing examples are from the First World War. From the Second World War the following are taken:

Supreme Headquarters, Allied Expeditionary Force: on a black shield, representing the darkness of Nazi oppression, a flaming sword for liberation and avenging justice, and above it a rainbow, emblematic of hope, containing all the colours of the allied flags.

First Army: a shield charged with the red cross of St. George and thereon a gold crusader's sword. The Second Army bore the same with the cross blue.

43rd (Wessex) Division: a gold wyvern on blue—being the ancient dragon of Wessex in the form in which it appears on the Bayeux Tapestry. This was a notable revival of an emblem which, as we have seen, was raised by the English at Hastings, in the Crusades, at Crécy, and at Agincourt (Chapter IV).

11th Anti-aircraft Division: the German eagle transfixed by an arrow.

Essex County Division: the three seaxes, white on red (see page 23).

London District: the red sword of St. Paul encircled by a gold mural crown, on a blue ground.

Northumberland District: a shield with gold and red vertical stripes as referred to on page 27 as the arms attributed to the Kingdom of Bernicia.

The old heraldic habit of punning quite properly found its place in this war-time heraldry. In the First World War the 19th Corps had as a sign three question marks in allusion to the name of its commander, Sir Herbert Watts. Lord Allenby's nickname, "Bull," accounted for the bull's-eye sign of the Third Army. Five rings joined together to form a cross, thus making four 8's, formed the badge of the 32nd Division. The 11th Corps placed the sign of a Corps Headquarters (a white cross on red) within a star of eleven points. The 5th Corps had a five-pointed star; the 21st Division three sevens arranged like a three-armed swastika; and the 67th six sevens similarly joined. The 61st used a monogram of the letters LXI, and the 18th the letters ATN.

War-time experiences found record in some of the signs, such as the broken spur of the 74th (Yeomanry) Division, adopted when they undertook infantry service. The 75th, who took a point regarded as the key to Jerusalem, adopted a key, and the 54th (East Anglian) used an umbrella turned inside out as a reminder that they turned the Turks out of Umbrella Hill, near Gaza.

Medal ribbons are another branch of war heraldry which deserve a note. The First World War Victory ribbon, with its red merging into green and violet on each side, symbolises the rainbow, indicating calm after storm, and perhaps hopefully referring to the Divine promise of the rainbow after the Flood.

The General Service Medal ribbon has the black and white of the Hohenzollerns hemmed in between blue and yellow for the English navy and army.

In token of their services to the nation a number of distinguished sailors and soldiers who received peerages were granted supporters telling of their achievements. Thus the Earl of Ypres was given two lions, one holding a Union Jack and the other a Belgian flag. A sailor and a marine maintain the shield of Earl Beatty, while above the beehive with nine bees on his blue shield is a chief containing the cross of St. George. Viscount Montgomery of Alamein has a knight in chain armour and a soldier in battle dress. Lord Portal of Hungerford has a pilot and a mechanic of the Royal Air Force in service dress, while an "astral crown," composed of stars between wings, forms part of his crest.

The Renaissance of Heraldry.

To-day the decorative and symbolic value of heraldry is recognised as never before, and there are many signs that the old art is coming more and more into contact with the everyday life of the twentieth century, and is being greeted with growing appreciation.

This is partly due to the great improvement in heraldic art during recent years, shown on some things in everyday use like stamps and coins. The 1927 issue of coins was much superior to that which preceded it, both as regards technical accuracy and artistic treatment. The vigorous lion on the new shillings illustrated how good heraldic design is drawing inspiration from old examples, while giving full scope to modern conception and taste. The restoration to the small silver of the oak, with its memories of King Charles's wanderings, and its significance of the survival of kingship in Great Britain, was also welcome; but the most striking change for the better was in the half-crown. Not only is this coin more dignified and graceful as regards the shield-form, but it is correct as to the Scottish tressure, which, in the previous issue, had all the fleurs-de-lys heads pointed outwards, instead of the alternate ones pointing towards the centre of the shield. While one may regret the disappearance of the Garter, one cannot

FIG. 250.—THE ROYAL ARMS BY
MR. REYNOLDS STONE.

regret the loss of the excessively long Garter which meandered tor-
tuously round the clumsy shield in the former half-crowns.

The significance of the denominations "crown" and "half-
crown" was renewed by the restoration of the royal crown to the five-
shilling-piece; and though one hears complaints at the removal of
the classic St. George (preserved, however, on the paper money), the
student of historic heraldry, accustomed to the fully-armed saint of
mediæval tradition, must feel that Pistrucci, who designed the St.
George of the nineteenth-century coinage, treated him shabbily by
turning him out clad only in a helmet and cloak to battle with the
dragon.

The coinage of King George VI's reign had several points of
heraldic interest, notably the Scottish shilling with the Royal Crest of
Scotland between St. Andrew's cross and the thistle, and the florin
with a crowned rose between a thistle and a shamrock-leaf.

In the reign of Queen Elizabeth II the practice of issuing two
distinct shillings has been continued, one with a shield bearing the
three lions of England and the other with a shield of the arms of
Scotland. In each case the shield is ensigned by the Royal Crown,
but this varies slightly in design. On the English shilling the arches
rise from behind the crosses on the rim (as they do in St. Edward's
Crown and the State Crown) while on the Scottish shillings they rise
from behind the fleurs-de-lys as in the case of the Crown of Scotland
preserved at Edinburgh Castle. Among other innovations in the

FIG. 251.—THE WEMBLEY LION

coinage of the present reign were the introduction of the leek for Wales, together with the rose, thistle and shamrock, on the crown-pieces, florins and sixpences, and also the old Tudor badge of a crowned portcullis (from the Beauforts) on the threepenny pieces.

On the postage stamps of Great Britain heraldry is not much used, because it is traditional that the Sovereign's head shall be the principal feature of the design, and emblems, where included, must take a secondary place. However, the Royal Arms, with finely drawn supporters, appear on the half-crown and five-shilling stamps, but the design suffers by a disproportionately small crown, necessary to leave space for the Sovereign's head above it. As on some of the coins, the rose, thistle and shamrock are used decoratively on the stamps, but they are accompanied by the daffodil, instead of the leek, for Wales.

A fine heraldic stamp is that issued in Southern Rhodesia in 1940, commemorating the Golden Jubilee of the British South Africa Company, and displaying the Company's arms.

Publicity display is making use of heraldry to an increasing extent. Royal Warrant holders, who are entitled to display the Royal Arms (and it is well to remember that anyone else doing so can be legally restrained), frequently take the trouble to have them carefully and accurately drawn for their advertisements. But occasionally one comes across firms who adhere slavishly to old-fashioned designs in which tame and over-fed beasts loll beside, rather than support, a florid shield surmounted by a disproportionate crown and crest. Newspapers which

FIG. 252.—THE RED LION,
COLCHESTER.

FIG. 253.—THE WHITE SWAN,
STRATFORD-ON-AVON

FIG. 254.—AN HERALDIC
TRADE EMBLEM.

display the Royal Arms in their titles are notable sinners in this respect. But Victorianism in heraldic art is less objectionable than the opposite extreme—namely, to conventionalise what is already conventional and thus produce a sort of impressionistic travesty of the Royal Arms. Impressionism applied to a single emblem of heraldic character may be striking and pleasing, witness the "Wembley lion" designed for the British Empire Exhibition (Fig. 251). But a coat-of-arms treated in the manner of the Wembley lion would so far transgress heraldic rules as to cease to be heraldry.

Artists may quite properly exercise their fancy and originality in depicting emblems and badges which, while heraldic in origin, are not subject to heraldic laws. An instance of the modern treatment of an old badge is shown in Fig. 252. This is the emblem of the Red Lion, Colchester, which perhaps derived it from John of Gaunt's badge of a red lion, adopted when he styled himself King of Castile and Leon. Another good inn sign is that of the White Swan at Stratford-on-Avon (Fig. 253), which represents the modern artist's version of the old Bohun badge illustrated in Table VI. The publicity device shown in Fig. 254 illustrates the way in which a national emblem may be legitimately and effectively used to convey the fact of British goods; the Union Jack sometimes appears in advertisements, but this is an incorrect use of the national flag and is particularly objectionable when it is made the background for a trade name or slogan.

Many trade-marks are definitely heraldic. We have remarked that King Robert Bruce's heart has found its way, *via* the arms of Douglas, on to a make of motor-cycles, and that the Kentish horse indicates a certain firm's steam rollers. Similarly the red hand of Ulster has been pressed into service by a brewery company whose head is a baronet. Reversing this process, some grantees of arms have adopted emblems recalling their commercial interests. One, whose name was associated with a group of teashops and provision stores, had for crest sprigs of tea and coffee. Another, whose name stood for malted milk, had bulls' heads and barley in his shield. Winged wheels appear in the arms of a cycle manufacturer. Although a coat-of-arms should be more than John Ridd (in *Lorna Doone*) would have made it, something with which "to stamp our pats of butter before they went to market," we may feel that arms which reflect their bearer's career and interests, even though purely commercial, are to-day as honourable as those which in feudal times expressed the unproductive industry of warfare.

Experts in heraldry have not always been tolerant of the modern trend which proves its continued vigour, and its contact with the present age. In an article in the *Morning Post* in 1926 Mr. Fox-Davies, while concluding that taken as a whole the arms being granted at the moment are good, commented on "silly supporters . . . like navvies and colliers and soldiers and marines," and charges "like building cranes and corrugated boiler-flues for those who want and insist upon them."

This called forth a protest from a writer in the *Manchester Guardian*:

"The odd thing about the modern heraldic expert is that he doesn't want modern heraldry to mean anything. . . . Would not two colliers, gules, protestant, make most appropriate supporters of a revised coat-of-arms granted to the Duke of Northumberland? . . . . Let us have a little common sense on this subject, and less of that fashionable cant about the Middle Ages. The able, acquisitive man takes the chance which his century affords him—Agincourt in one age, an advertising agency in another. Many a lad who would have been knocking peasants on the head in France five hundred years ago is now trying to corner their food on a Stock Exchange. If he brings it off, why grudge him a bull and a bear for the supporters of his coat-of-arms? No reason at all, except that it has been decided that 'modern heraldry' shall have less real significance than the samplers our great-grandmothers used to work."

Flippancies aside, the writer reflects a popular point of view which must be reckoned with, especially in a book which seeks to represent heraldry in a popular manner. While both art and tradition must condemn the corrugated boiler-flue (which was actually granted to the late Samson Fox of Leeds and Harrogate) and similar charges, if heraldry is to be a living art with a part to play in the twentieth century scientific and industrial achievements must not be denied a place among the things which it commemorates. The true tradition of heraldry is not to dwell in the past, but to move with the times. Swords and helmets, waterskins and pilgrims' staves, beacons and battering-rams were all modern and utilitarian objects when they were introduced into coats-of-arms. Shields designed at various periods contain the ancient "lymphad," ships of the fifteenth and sixteenth centuries, wooden walls of Nelson's day, and a paddle-wheel steamer under steam and sail—the last being in the arms of Barrow-in-Furness. The doors of the heraldic menagerie have been opened to the birds and beasts of the new continents; exotic flowers and trees have supplemented the limited flora of old armory; and why should not devices representing science, industry and commerce take their place in coats-of-arms?

The objection apparently is not to the principle of expressing modern facts and achievements in terms of heraldry, but to the offence against heraldic art and convention which such a charge as a boiler-flue commits. It is obvious that such articles should be reduced to essentials and translated into symbolic forms. For instance, Sir John Herschel's forty-foot reflecting telescope, complete with apparatus, is an unsuitable charge: a mass of detail, it defies illustration in so limited a space as a shield affords; but the heralds might have perpetuated the memory of his life's work more subtly and with greater regard for the traditions of their craft if they had given him a blue shield with one large silver star encircled by a gold ring, between three small stars—the large one representing the magnifying effect of the

Q

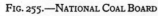

FIG. 255.—NATIONAL COAL BOARD

FIG. 256.—ATOMIC ENERGY
AUTHORITY.

telescope.   Similarly a road-making plant would not, from the point
of view of heraldic art, be a pleasant coat-of-arms for a highway
engineer, but three winged wheels on a pale or bend, indicating the
speedy road traffic which his work facilitated, would be both symbolic
and artistic.   An excellent instance of the conventional treatment of
scientific appliances is the flame encompassed by a chain granted to
Sir Humphry Davy to commemorate his invention of the safety lamp.
    Some articles connected with new inventions are in themselves
sufficiently graceful and simple as to be suitable heraldic emblems.
But, as a rule, in expressing the facts of modern science the old
heraldic forms will have to be employed with new significance.   We
have already the rod of Æsculapius (a staff entwined by a serpent) to
stand for medical skill, and there is no need to introduce the stetho-
scope or scalpel; the fetterlock is a fine symbol of security, and need
not give place to the safe with combination lock; and the water budget
can still be regarded as adequate to express the idea of water supply,
and does not need to be supplemented by tanks and reservoirs.
    Some recent grants of arms to public bodies illustrate the point.

The shield of the National Coal Board (Fig. 255) effectively conveys the idea of getting coal above the surface by a simple design using only traditional forms.   The arms of the United Kingdom Atomic Energy Authority (Fig. 256), while more elaborate, are also composed entirely of old heraldic forms and charges used with a new meaning.   In the shield the white roundels on black represent a block of graphite with uranium rods inserted in it.   The heraldic pile (see Fig. 4) is used to stand for the atomic pile, and its "dancetty" (or zigzag) design of gold and red suggests nuclear fission generating energy.   The crest shows the sun, the source of heat and energy, with emblems from the arms of Lord Rutherford, the pioneer of atomic research.   The supporters are two pantheons spotted with gold stars, collared and chained.   The pantheon is a rare heraldic creature which was little known until it was introduced into these arms to represent natural forces in the universe. They are collared (with crowns composed of palisades) and chained to show the forces are under control.   Each pantheon has thirteen six-pointed and two seven-pointed stars, the number of points adding up to ninety-two, this being the atomic number of uranium.

In this survey of heraldry, which seeks rather to arouse interest than to convey knowledge, no attempt has been made to review the subject from any other standpoint than that of the general reader of British history, and only passing reference has been made to its value to the specialist in archæology or genealogy.   Those who desire to go more deeply into the art, whether as an aid to historical studies or for its own sake, must turn not only to more scholarly books, but also to armorial records, monumental brasses and tombs, the ancient churches and other buildings which are wealthy in heraldic work.   So far as this book is concerned, its purpose has been achieved if the reader, having followed it so far with interest, closes it with the impression that heraldry is worth his attention, whether the careful observation of the student or the more casual notice of the rambler in the field of history. Of great antiquity in its origin, and in every age receptive to fresh sources of beauty and vigour, heraldry has grown continually in depth of meaning and breadth of appeal, and in these swiftly-changing days we may value it as one of those silent influences which combine to link the centuries in the chain of tradition.

INDEX